IS-303: Radiological Accident Assessment Concepts

By

Fema

1/13/2014

Lesson 1: The Nuclear Reactor Process and Commercial Reactors

Course Welcome

This Independent Study course is a prerequisite for the resident EMI classroom course "Radiological Accident Assessment Concepts." As such, this Independent Study course provides only an overview of key concepts that will be addressed in more depth in the classroom course.

In this course you will learn how to assess the off-site radiological consequences to the public following a release of radioactivity from nuclear power reactors and non-reactor incidents and how to use this assessment as a basis for recommending protective actions to decision makers.

Please note that this course will take approximately **16 hours** to complete. It is recommended that you plan on taking the course in multiple sittings.

Course Objectives

At the end of this course, you will be able to:

- Describe the source and magnitude of the threat to the public from a nuclear power plant incident.
- Describe preventive and protective measures which may be implemented to protect the public and emergency workers during a nuclear incident, and use the Federal guidance to determine when each of these measures is necessary or appropriate.
- Describe the relationship of dose and dose pathway to the Environmental Protection Agency (EPA) protective action guides (PAGs), early injuries, and early deaths.
- Describe the guidelines and recommendations associated with using potassium iodide as a supplemental public protective action.
- Describe suggested protective actions for milk, fruits and vegetables, meat and meat products, poultry and poultry products, soils, grains, and water.
- Explain the appropriate techniques, procedures, and available Federal agency capabilities and resources to gather and assess data during and after a nuclear or radiological incident.
- Convert from International System of Units (SI) to customary units and customary units to SI using a hand calculator.
- Use a hand calculator to solve problems using the equations used throughout the course.

Screen Features
- Click on the Course Menu button to access the menu listing all lessons of this course. You can select any of the lessons from this menu by simply clicking on the lesson title.
- Click on the Glossary button to look up key definitions and acronyms.
- Click on the Help button to review guidance and troubleshooting advice regarding navigating through the course.

- Track your progress by looking at the Progress bar at the top right of each screen. To see a numeric display, roll your mouse over the Progress bar area.
- Follow the bolded green instructions that appear on each screen in order to proceed to the next screen or complete a Knowledge Review or Activity.
- Click on the Back or the Next buttons at the top and bottom of screens to move backward or forward in the lesson. Note: If the Next button is dimmed, you must complete an activity before you can proceed in the lesson.

Navigating Using Your Keyboard

Below are instructions for navigating through the course using your keyboard.

- Use the "Tab" key to move forward through each screen's navigation buttons and hyperlinks, or "Shift" + "Tab" to move backwards. A box surrounds the button that is currently selected.
- Press "Enter" to select a navigation button or hyperlink.
- Use the arrow keys to select answers for multiple-choice review questions or self-assessment checklists. Then tab to the "Submit" button and press "Enter" to complete a Knowledge Review or Self-Assessment.

Warning: Repeatedly pressing "Tab" beyond the number of selections on the screen may cause the keyboard to lock up. Use "Ctrl" + "Tab" to deselect an element or reset to the beginning of a screen's navigation links (most often needed for screens with animations or media).

- JAWS assistive technology users can press the Ctrl key to quiet the screen reader while the course audio plays.

Receiving Credit

To receive credit for this course, you must:

Complete all of the lessons. Each lesson will take between 30 minutes and 1 hour to complete.

Remember . . . YOU MUST COMPLETE THE ENTIRE COURSE TO RECEIVE CREDIT. If you have to leave the course, do not exit from the course or close your browser. If you exit from the course, you will need to start that lesson over again.

Pass the final exam. The last screen provides instructions on how to complete the final exam.

Lesson Overview

The purpose of this lesson is to introduce the course and provide a basic overview of the nuclear reactor process, commercial reactors, and consequences of radiation exposure.

Upon completion of this lesson, you will be able to:
- Describe the threat to the public health from a nuclear power plant accident.
- Describe the basic plant systems.

You can access the glossary in one of two ways throughout this course. You can select the glossary button in the top right hand corner of each main content screen. In addition, on content screens you can select underlined words to access their definitions in the online glossary. Selecting an underlined word will take you directly to its definition in the glossary.

This lesson should take approximately **35 minutes** to complete.

Radiological Accident Assessments

The primary goal of radiological accident assessment is to ensure public protection in the event of a reactor emergency. Specifically, the goals are to:
- Reduce the risk or mitigate an accident at its source.
- Reduce the risk of serious deterministic health effects (deaths).
- Reduce the risk of stochastic effects (cancers).

Effects of Radiation Exposure

Radiation exposure can cause many negative health effects. These effects include:
- Deterministic effects. These are defined as prompt radiation effects (observable within a short period of time), the severity of which varies with the dose and for which a practical threshold exists.
- Stochastic effects. These refer to those effects whose chance of occurrence increases in proportion to exposure—in this case, cancer. The severity is not proportional to the dose (e.g., you either get or don't get cancer). There may be no threshold dose.

Under normal operations, public exposure to radiation from nuclear reactors is minimal because of barriers between the public and the radioactive material; however, during a nuclear incident, the source of exposure to the public is not under control.

Now that you have learned about the health risks of radiation exposure, let's explore the ways in which the EPA protects the public during nuclear incidents.

Protective Action Guides (PAGs)

The Environmental Protection Agency (EPA) has established protective action guides (PAGs) for the principal phases of a nuclear incident. The public usually can be protected in the case of a nuclear incident by some form of intervention that will disrupt normal living. Such intervention is called protective action.

PAGs help public officials make protective decisions during a nuclear incident. Specifically, they outline the projected dose to a standard man (e.g., reference man) or other defined individual from an unplanned release of radioactive material, and the level at which a specific protective action to reduce or avoid that dose is warranted. They are based on estimates of cancer risks (risk of someone dying from cancer).

Let's examine the primary protective action objective.

Preventing Deterministic Health Effects

The primary protective action objective is to prevent deterministic health effects from radiation exposure. The best way to do this is to pay attention to what is happening in the nuclear power plant. Initially, protective actions should be based on plant conditions such as status of the reactor, critical safety functions, and fission product barriers, all of which you will learn about later. Protective actions should not be delayed until dose projections are made.

You learned earlier that the severity of deterministic health effects varies. Next, you will learn about the source of the most severe case: death.

Source of Exposure

For reactor accidents, the most likely source of death is bone marrow exposure, which may come from:

- The passing plume
- Ground contamination
- Dose due to inhalation

Now that you've learned about the potential dangers of reactor incidents and the importance of public protection, let's examine the basics of the nuclear reactor process and ways in which public exposure can occur.

Fission and the Nuclear Reactor Process

Nuclear power plants produce electricity. This process is produced through fission — the splitting apart of atoms. Split atoms generate energy in the form of heat.

The heat energy produced from fission is used to convert water to steam, and the steam produces electricity.

Now that you have learned about the basics of the nuclear reactor process and the definition of fission, let's examine how nuclear plants induce fission on uranium.

Fission: Uranium

The element used in the reactor core is uranium. The majority of power in a nuclear plant comes from uranium in two ways:

- The fission of uranium-235 (U-235)
- The conversion of uranium-238 (U-238) to plutonium which then fissions

Fission: U-235

U-235 is the uranium isotope that fissions with a thermal neutron, a slow travelling neutron. For the fission process to occur, a thermal neutron strikes a U-235 atom. The U-235 atom then absorbs the neutron. The fission splits the U-235 atom and yields two fission products and releases several neutrons, typically two to three, and energy, mostly in the form of heat.

Without artificial enhancement, uranium, as it naturally occurs (natural-enrichment uranium), contains only 0.72% U-235, which is insufficient to sustain the fission process. A procedure called enrichment is used to raise the percentage from the 0.72% found in nature to 3-5% required for effective use in the core.

U-238 as a Fuel

Another source of fuel comes from the neutron absorption of U-238. A decay process involving U-238 yields a plutonium isotope (Pu-239). This becomes a significant contribution to the reactor's fuel after the reactor has been operating, because it mimics U-235 and can absorb neutrons. Late in core life, the plutonium fissions can account for up to 30% of the reactor power.

The image below shows the fission of U-235 after absorption of a thermal neutron.

Now that you've learned about the ways in which power comes from the fission of uranium, let's find out how this power is harnessed and used within a nuclear reactor.

How Fuel is used in a Reactor

Uranium dioxide (UO2) powder is shaped into small, cylindrical ceramic pellets, less than a half-inch high, by high-pressure cold compression. Once the pellets have been shaped, they are heated at very high temperatures to form a ceramic material. Being ceramic, the UO2 pellets are resistant to interaction with water and are chemically inert to the reactor fuel rod (cladding) at operating temperatures.

The fuel pellets are stacked inside hollow tubes made of zirconium alloy, called fuel rods. The fuel rods are loaded with natural-enrichment fuel pellets, and the remaining space is filled with various concentrations of fuel enrichment. Natural-enrichment UO2 pellets are loaded in the top and bottom of the fuel rods of the central core bundles and in the entire length of the peripheral fuel bundles to act as a neutron reflector at the core boundary.

Fission Products

When a neutron strikes a U-235 atom, the U-235 atom absorbs it. This makes the nucleus of the U-235 atom unstable and causes it to split into two or more lighter atoms called fission products (fission fragments). At the same time, energy in the form of heat is released along with two or three neutrons. The neutrons can strike other uranium atoms and cause additional fissions. The continuing process of fission is known as a chain reaction.

Neutron Losses (1 of 2)

As you already learned, for the fission process to occur, the initiating neutrons must be at low energy (that is, traveling slowly). These are thermal neutrons.

The neutrons released during the fission process are at very high energy. These high-energy or fast-traveling neutrons must be slowed down through collisions with core materials or coolant to become thermal. While the fast neutrons are being slowed down, there are several possible ways for them to interact.

They can leak out of the core, be absorbed by structural material, or be absorbed in the coolant. Even if a neutron is absorbed by a U-235 nucleus, it may not cause fission if its energy level is still too high at the time it is absorbed. The manipulation of these neutron losses is used to control the reactor power level.

Neutron Losses (2 of 2)

If every fission releases one neutron that slows down and causes another fission, the rate of fission will remain constant. This is a stable chain reaction and the reactor is said to be critical.

If the number of fissions is increasing, the reactor is supercritical. A supercritical reactor's power level is increasing.

If the neutron losses are greater than the gains from fission, the reactor is subcritical, and the power level is decreasing.

Fission Product Poisons

Some fission products are called fission product poisons because they absorb neutrons. As fission product poisons build up, they reduce the reactor's power by making neutrons unavailable for fission.

Some poisons are intentionally added to the fuel, allowing more fuel to be initially loaded in the core. These are called burnable poisons. Poisons can also be added in regions of the core to even out power generation.

Control Rods

Control rods, which are positioned in the core to control the reactor, are actually poison rods that absorb neutrons to lower the reactor's power level. In an emergency, these rods are rapidly and automatically inserted into the core to stop the chain reaction. Liquid poisons, such as boron, may also be injected in an emergency to stop the fission process.

After a reactor is shut down, the core continues to produce decay heat from the decay of radioactive fission products as well as the dwindling number of fissions. Even when the reactor is subcritical, it can be producing up to about 7% of rated reactor power due to decay heat for a few hours. This is the reason post shut down cooling systems are given so much emphasis.

Types of Commercial Reactors

In the next section of this lesson, you will learn about commercial reactors.

There are two types of nuclear power plants in the United States. Two-thirds of the plants are pressurized water reactors (PWRs); the remaining third are boiling water reactors (BWRs).

Boiling Water Reactors (BWRs)

The Boiling Water Reactor, or BWR, operates in essentially the same way as a fossil-fueled generating plant. Inside the reactor vessel, heat from the fission of uranium fuel in the reactor core boils coolant water into steam. The steam travels through a moisture separator and is piped to the turbine, which turns the electrical generator. The steam is condensed back into water in the condenser. The water is then pumped back to the reactor vessel to be reboiled. The recirculation pumps and jet pumps take a portion of the coolant water and reinject it into the reactor vessel to increase the mixing and flow of reactor coolant. The reactor vessel and recirculation pumps are located inside the containment.

Pressurized Water Reactors (PWRs)

Although they both have reactor vessels, the Pressurized Water Reactor, or PWR, differs from the Boiling Water Reactor in that steam is produced in the steam generator rather than in the reactor vessel. The pressurizer keeps the reactor coolant (water) under very high pressure (about 2200 pounds per square inch) to prevent it from boiling, even at operating temperatures of 600 degrees F.

Lesson Summary

Let's summarize what you learned in this lesson:

- The main goal of radiological accident assessment is to ensure public protection.
- Radiation exposure can cause deterministic and stochastic effects.
- Protective Action Guides (PAGs) help public officials make protective decisions during a nuclear incident.
- Nuclear power plants produce electricity by using fission to generate heat. The heat energy is used to convert water to steam, and the steam produces electricity.
- There are two types of nuclear power plants in the United States: pressurized water reactors (PWRs) and boiling water reactors (BWRs).

The next lesson will cover plant stability: what failures must occur to cause major off-site consequences and the components of plant systems designed to control such a threat.

Lesson 2: Plant Stability

Lesson Overview

The purpose of this lesson is to examine the events during a reactor accident that could potentially cause public radiation exposure. This lesson also covers components of plant systems designed to control the threat of exposure.

Upon completion of this lesson, you will be able to:

- Describe what failures must occur to cause major off-site consequences.
- Describe the components of plant systems designed to control the threat of major off-site consequences.

Remember you can access the glossary in one of two ways throughout this course. You can select the glossary button in the top right hand corner of each main content screen. In addition, on content screens you can select underlined words to access their definitions in the online glossary. Selecting an underlined word will take you directly to its definition in the glossary.

This lesson should take approximately **35 minutes** to complete.

Radioactivity of Fission Products

In Lesson 1, you learned that when a neutron strikes a U-235 atom, the U-235 atom absorbs it. This makes the nucleus of the U-235 atom unstable and causes it to split into two or more lighter atoms called fission products.

Fission products are radioactive and must be kept inside the reactor. The fission process must be stopped and the reactor shut down if there is an accident. When the reactor shuts down, heat is still being produced by fission products. Even when the reactor is shut down, the accident is not yet over and damage could continue.

Exposure Prevention Systems

During a reactor shutdown, the plant must keep the radioactivity in, but let the heat out. Heat causes pressure to build up. To protect the containment, heat must be removed.

The plant's safety systems begin operating after the reactor is shut down.

There are two types of exposure prevention systems:

- Passive systems that contain the fission products
- Active systems that keep the barriers cool and control decay heat

Next you will learn what occurs after a reactor shutdown.

After Reactor Shutdown

Within the first hour after shutdown, heat decreases rapidly. There is a 25% drop in temperature. This is the most critical period of an accident and the one in which the most stress is placed on safety mechanisms.

One month after the accident, heat decreases level off, and a further drop in temperature occurs. This is still an area of concern because heat must continue to be removed over the long term and fission products may still be unstable.

Next you'll learn about the main source of radiation exposure to the public.

Radiation Exposure to the Public

The only location in the plant that contains enough radioiodine to pose off-site health risks is the core. It contains enough radioactive iodine (radioiodine) to cause deterministic health effects. Releasing 1 or 2% of the radioiodine within the core directly into the atmosphere creates the possibility of early health effects off-site.

Therefore, severe reactor core damage is the main event that can lead to radiation exposure of the public. This is what occurred at Three Mile Island. A combination of operator error and equipment malfunction permitted the core to become uncovered, overheat, partially melt, and release large quantities of radioactive material into the containment. While there was severe core damage at Three Mile Island, offsite exposures were very low due to the fact that the containment did its job and did not fail.

Containment Failure

After core damage has occurred, the containment structure must be protected. There are four general areas of containment failure:

- Overpressurization
- Bypass

- Direct containment heating
- Containment venting

In the next section of this lesson, you will learn about these four types of containment failure.

Overpressurization (1 of 2)

If decay heat from the core is being released into the containment and is not being removed, the pressure could cause containment failure. This decay heat must be removed for several days to weeks after reactor shutdown.

U.S. commercial reactor containments have a design leak rate of 0.1–0.25% per day at design pressure.

Most containments fail at two to three times the pressure at which they were designed to operate. It takes over 20 hours for overpressure failures due to decay heat to occur. Decay heat can be removed by:

- Sprays or containment coolers.
- Venting to release pressure.

Overpressurization (2 of 2)

Hydrogen (H2) may be produced during core damage and must be controlled by preventing the Zircaloy-water reaction. Containments at very high pressure have insufficient oxygen to allow an H2 burn. This is called inerting. In some accidents, the inerting could be lost through containment leakage. Steam can also inert a containment until the sprays come on and remove the steam. The containment can also be vented to release the excess H2.

Containment Bypass

Bypassing allows a release of radioactive materials directly from the reactor coolant system into an area outside the containment. Releases may be monitored or unmonitored. The releases may also be unfiltered, allowing iodines and particulates to escape along with krypton and xenon (noble gases). The following would cause the containment to be bypassed:

- A steam generator tube rupture (SGTR) in a PWR
- Failure to isolate the main steam lines in a BWR
- Loss-of-coolant accident (LOCA) outside of containment

Direct Containment Heating

Direct containment heating (DCH) is the collective term for everything that can happen if the core melts through the bottom of the reactor vessel—a large increase in pressure and the production of large amounts of hydrogen. Direct containment heating is possible for hours after core damage. Although this did not happen at TMI, some models indicate that the reactor vessel should have failed during the accident.

Containment Venting

Power plants have procedures for venting the containment to remove hydrogen and to release pressure. Containment venting does not consider the radioactive dose that the population may have received from any previous release that may have taken place. To prevent a very large dose due to containment failure, a smaller dose through venting may present an acceptable risk to those making the decision. Consequently, venting could result in a substantial dose off-site.

As you learned earlier in the lesson, there are many ways in which the containment can fail. Venting is predictable; however, failure is not.

Now that you know how radiation exposure can occur, let's review the barriers designed to protect the public.

Fission Product Barriers

You just learned about the four general areas of containment failure.

Next, you will learn about the three main fission product barriers designed to keep nuclear fission products away from the population:

- Cladding (fuel rods or pins)
- The reactor coolant system (RCS)
- The containment structure

On the next screens, you will learn about each of these fission product barriers.

Cladding (1 of 2)

Cladding around the fuel rods or fuel pins is the first and most important barrier. Fuel rods are made of zirconium alloy (Zircaloy) and the material from which the tubes are made is known as cladding.

Once filled with uranium fuel pellets, the tubes are pressurized with helium gas and sealed. As the reactor operates, gaseous fission products are generated and collect in the fuel rod.

Cladding (2 of 2)

Approximately 5% of the cesium, iodine, and noble gases created by fission are contained in the top of the fuel rod, an area referred to as the gap. If radioactivity in the gap is released into the reactor coolant, a gap release has occurred.

From time to time, cladding imperfection may occur resulting in the release from that particular rod. A major gap release is evidence of a serious reactor accident. The probability of a reactor undergoing a major gap release is in the order of 1 in 1,000,000 over its lifetime.

To prevent the fuel rods from failing and releasing radioactive materials into the coolant, always keep the fuel covered with water. Water transfers the heat away from the fuel rods. Excessive heat can damage the rods.

Reactor Coolant System (1 of 2)

The reactor coolant system (RCS) or primary system is the plumbing that goes around the fuel and acts as the second barrier against a release of radioactive products. This system holds the water that cools the core. Core damage can occur only if it fails. In the event of a reactor failure, this system is not 100% reliable because it has many possible failure points.

Reactor Coolant System (2 of 2)

The location at which an RCS fails provides indicators of the type of release that can be expected. It also indicates how you can keep the core covered in water. All RCSs have pilot-operated relief valves (PORVs) and safety valves that are designed to open during an accident.

Containment Structure

The containment structure encases the rods, plumbing, and water and acts as the third barrier against radioactive release. It should capture any release that makes it past the first two barriers. It is designed to:

- Withstand the large increase in pressure resulting from a break in the RCS (called a blowdown).
- Reduce the amount of fission products released into the environment during an accident.
- Remove the long-term heat generated by fission products as they decay.

If the containment structure does not fail or leak abnormally, there will be very low dose off-site in the event of an accident, even if the reactor sustains very severe core damage. This was observed at Three Mile Island (TMI).

Let's examine containment designs for pressurized water reactors (PWRs) and boiling water reactors (BWRs).

Pressurized Water Reactor (PWR) Containment Designs (1 of 2)

There are several types of containment designs.

PWR containments are large, strong concrete rooms that contain the reactor plumbing. Their size and strength, as well as other features, such as sprays, suppression pools, and ice vats, that wash fission products and remove heat, enable them to withstand blowdowns. The heat removal process occurs on a long-term basis.

Pressurized Water Reactor (PWR) Containment Designs (2 of 2)

Some PWR containment designs use ice to condense steam, thereby keeping the containment pressure low during an accident. This may also be accompanied by containment sprays (a feature found in PWRs and BWRs), which are also used to condense steam.

Boiling Water Reactor (BWR) Containment Designs

Older boiling water reactor (BWR) containments are very small and have suppression pools where the steam is condensed and fission products are filtered. Later-generation BWR containments resemble PWR high-pressure containments—large and robust. BWR containments also have sprays to reduce pressure by condensing gases. Some BWR containments employ hydrogen igniters near the top of containment to control-burn hydrogen, which may be generated by a Zircaloy-water reaction during an accident.

Three major containment types were created during the evolution of BWR containments.

- BWR Mark I Containment Design
- BWR Mark II Containment Design
- BWR Mark III Containment Design

Predicting containment performance is difficult. You won't know when containment will fail until it does.

Critical Safety Function (CSF) Overview

You just learned about fission product barriers. In the next section of the lesson, you will learn about critical safety functions (CSFs).

CSFs are actions that were developed to:

- Protect the integrity of the fission product barriers.
- Allow emergency operations during accident conditions.
- Outline what has to be done, independent of the nature of a failure, to protect the containment and the core.

The following questions should be asked in this order to ensure that CSFs are adequately maintained:

- Is the reactor shut down?
- Is the core covered with water? How? How do you know?
- How is the decay heat being removed? To where? How do you know?
- What is the status of the vital auxiliaries (AC and DC power) and how do you know?

CSF #1: Shut Down the Reactor

Shutting down the reactor is the first and most important CSF.

The reactor protection system (RPS) is used to shut down, or scram, the reactor. This is accomplished by the rapid insertion of control rods to stop the fission. Control rods are materials that are neutron poisons; they absorb neutrons. Boron may also be injected to absorb neutrons.

It is crucial that the reactor be shut down during an accident because the safety systems are not designed to perform their functions while the reactor is operating, the reactor must be shut down.

If the reactor fails to shut down, you must rely on its emergency cooling systems. Failure of the automatic system to shut down is called anticipated transient without scram (ATWS).

CSF #2: Keep the Core Covered and Cool (1 of 3)

The second CSF is to keep the core covered and cool. Water is used to remove the heat generated by the fission within the core. Failure to remove the heat can lead to fuel pin damage and RCS failure.

A break in the RCS will lead to water loss, which will cause the core to be uncovered if the water is not replaced. An uncovered core will heat up at 1°–2° F per second (0.5° -1° C/sec) and eventually cause fuel clad failure and release of fission products.

When the core temperature rises to between 1,400 and 2,000 degrees, between 15 and 20 minutes after the core is uncovered, the zirconium metal of the fuel rods reacts with the water cooling the core. This reaction produces hydrogen, which accelerates the temperature increase in the core. This is known as the Zircaloy-water reaction.

CSF #2: Keep the Core Covered and Cool (2 of 3)

If there is no injection of coolant into the containment structure, after 15 to 45 minutes, there could be:

- Cladding failure.
- Hydrogen gas generation.
- Gap release.
- Local fuel melt in the uncovered core.

After 30 to 90 minutes of being uncovered, the core may be uncoolable and:

- There may be rapid release of volatile fission products.
- The molten core may also slump to the bottom of the vessel.

After one to three or more hours, the core may melt through the vessel. There may also be

- Maximum core melt and hydrogen gas formation.
- Maximum in-vessel release of fission products.

CSF #2: Keep the Core Covered and Cool (3 of 3)

The emergency core cooling system (ECCS) is utilized to keep the core cool and covered. In the early phase of an incident, high- and low-pressure injection pumps supply coolant to the reactor. Water is initially supplied from storage tanks and then from recirculation of water from containment. The heat is removed from the core and released into containment.

CSF #3: Remove Decay Heat

The third CSF is removing decay heat. For long-term cooling, hot water (potentially containing radioactive material) is pumped from containment to heat exchangers, releasing the heat to the environment.

CSF #4: Maintain Vital Auxiliaries

The last CSF is to maintain vital auxiliaries. AC and DC power and console control must be maintained in order to read instruments, to operate pumps and valves to inject water, and to allow other safety features to function. Emergency diesel generators and batteries are vital auxiliaries.

As you will learn in this course, the loss of vital auxiliaries was critical in the Fukushima nuclear incident.

Other CSFs

Other CSFs include:

- Controlling the containment pressure through use of sprays, ice, and venting
- Controlling hydrogen buildup in containment through the use of igniters and recombiners

- Maintaining containment integrity
- Preventing direct containment heating from reactor vessel melt-through by such means as containment flooding

Lesson Summary

Let's summarize what you have learned in this lesson:

- Severe reactor core damage is the main event that can lead to radiation exposure of the public.
- There are four general areas of containment failure:
    - Overpressurization
    - Bypass
    - Direct containment heating
    - Containment venting
- There are three main fission product barriers designed to keep nuclear fission products away from the population:
    - Cladding (fuel rods or pins)
    - Reactor coolant system
    - Containment structure
- There are four main critical safety functions (CSFs): Shutting down the reactor
    - Keeping the core covered and cool
    - Removing decay heat
    - Maintaining vital auxiliaries

The next lesson will cover core damage assessment and release assessment.

Lesson 3: Core Damage and Release Assessment

Lesson Overview

The purpose of this lesson is to provide an overview of core damage and release assessment, as they relate to the complexity of monitoring release.

Upon completion of this lesson, you will be able to:

- Identify the indicators of core damage.
- Describe the two types of releases.
- Explain why an accurate computer modeling of a release is difficult.

Remember you can access the glossary in one of two ways throughout this course. You can select the glossary button in the top right hand corner of each main content screen. In addition, on content screens you can select underlined words to access their definitions in the online glossary. Selecting an underlined word will take you directly to its definition in the glossary.

This lesson should take approximately **35 minutes** to complete.

Types of Assessments

There are two types of assessments:

- Core damage assessment
- Release assessment

In the next section of this lesson, you will learn about core damage assessment as well as the indicators of core damage.

Indicators of Core Damage (1 of 2)

Indicators of core damage include the following:

- A critical safety function is lost.
- The cooling capabilities are impaired.
- Pressurized water reactor (PWR) core exit thermocouples indicate high temperatures.
- Water level is below the top of the core.
- Containment monitors show elevated radiation readings.
- Coolant or containment air samples show high activity.

Indicators of Core Damage (2 of 2)

There are key indicators that predict or indicate core damage.

- Safety Function Status:
    - predicts core damage
- Water injection:
    - predicts core damage
- Water level:
    - indicates imminent core damage
    - not measured in many PWRs
    - measured BWRs
- PWR core temperature
    - Indicates imminent core damage
    - Measured in PWRs
    - Not measured in BWRs
- Radiation levels:
    - confirm core damage

Note that some of the indicators are measured in PWRs only and others in boiling water reactors (BWRs) only.

Progression of an Incident

Now that you have learned about indicators of core damage, you will find out how an accident can progress from failure to atmospheric release.

Three Mile Island Unit 2 (TMI-2) Accident: Introduction

In the next few screens you will learn about the accident at Three Mile Island Unit 2 (TMI-2) nuclear power plant and how this accident is an example of core damage assessment.

TMI-2: Instruments

Instruments showed radiation levels in the plant at TMI. Within the first hour of the accident, numerous indicators of core damage went unrecognized.

Remember that radiation levels will increase in plant after core damage.

Officials did not know how instruments would act under accident conditions. Their confusion resulted in problems such as the following:

- Samples were not representative.
- Instruments were not read correctly.
- Instruments were not calibrated correctly.

TMI-2: Core Damage Indicators

Officials did not see the "big picture" or recognize the emerging pattern. Many things were going wrong simultaneously and, in general, readings were going up. Officials should have realized that the reactor was failing, but they did not.

Clear indicators of core damage were:

- Containment monitor radiation readings of 6,000 R/hr
- Core exit thermocouple temperature of 2,000° F (cladding failure at 1,200° F)

Instruments can be confusing during accidents. Therefore, never use a single instrument as a basis for assessment.

TMI-2: Core Damage

Within an hour, numerous process monitors were rising by factors of ten. Officials should have realized that core damage had occurred, but were confused by instrumentation problems noted earlier.

Officials did not realize they had melted material, between 20 and 40 tons, at the bottom of the containment vessel. After they realized the core was uncovered, they re-covered this material with water.

TMI-2 Conclusions

The Presidential Commission looking into the TMI accident found that:

- There was an incredible amount of radioactivity inside the containment.

- Plant authorities did not know what was happening.
- Plant authorities took no protective action.
- Under current criteria, people would be evacuated between five and ten miles around the plant.
- Many residents living around the plant voluntarily evacuated in an orderly manner.

Fukushima Nuclear Incident: Introduction

Now that you have learned about the Three Mile Island incident, you will find out what happened during the Fukushima nuclear incident.

The Tohoku earthquake, which occurred on Friday, March 11, 2011 on the east coast of northern Japan, is believed to be one of the largest earthquakes in recorded history, and the largest earthquake ever recorded in Japan. The earthquake and following tsunami resulted in over 19,000 deaths, inundated about 560 square kilometers, and caused $500 billion or more in damage and economic loss in Japan.

Fukushima Nuclear Incident: Progression of Events

Fifteen nuclear power reactors at five sites were in the area affected by the earthquake and tsunami. Eleven of these reactors were operating at the time of the earthquake, ten of them at full power. All of the operating reactors shut down automatically in response to the seismic activity. The earthquake and following tsunami caused disruption to all 15 reactors, ranging from partial loss of off-site power to complete loss of off-site and on-site power. The most severely affected plants were those at Fukushima Daiichi and Fukushima Daini.

Release Assessment

In the next section of this lesson you will learn about release assessment and what the incidents at Chernobyl and Fukushima have taught us about how to conduct this type of assessment.

Estimating the release rate and time is important, because they are the basis for dose projection. In order to calculate a dose to a population, parameters such as estimated release rate and duration are necessary. If the rates are unknown, calculations should be made using the upper and lower bounds of the range of possibilities.

Let's explore the two types of release characteristics:
- Unpredictability
- Unusual characteristics

Unpredictability (1 of 3)

The source term is an estimate of the composition, rate, timing, and elevation of a release from a nuclear power plant.

Accurately estimating the source term is difficult because:

- It is difficult to estimate the release characteristics – composition (isotopic mixture), rate (Ci/s or Bq/s), time release will begin, and elevation.
- There are very large uncertainties, especially with severe accidents.

Unpredictability (2 of 3)

There are two types of releases:

- Monitored releases - Monitored releases pose a lower threat to health, since a large portion of the most dangerous fission products will be removed by filters through which the release must pass on its way out of the plant, as long as the filters remain intact. Monitored release could also be reduced by plate-out (which refers to the depositing of radioiodine and other fission products on the cooler surfaces of the containment). If the filters fail, this monitored release would pose a higher threat.
- Unmonitored releases - Unmonitored releases pose a higher threat of inflicting early deterministic health effects on the population in their path since they arise from conditions such as containment failure or bypass. Unmonitored releases may result in early health effects. Estimates of release rate and composition are very uncertain for an unmonitored release. Most major releases would probably:
    - Be unpredictable.
    - Occur at unmonitored points.

Unpredictability (3 of 3)

The Nuclear Regulatory Commission (NRC) has expended large amounts of money and effort to assess both what is released during an accident and where it will go. The accuracy of estimates remains questionable because of the large number of variables involved.

It is necessary to verify projections using actual environmental measurements. These measurements will dictate whether additional protective actions need to be taken.

Unusual Characteristics

In the event of a major release, the usual characteristics of a release should be considered:

- Timing
    - 30 minutes to 24 hours after core damage
    - Last hours to days
- Rate profile
    - Very rapid at first, slowing down, and continuing for a long time
    - Small release whenever the core is damaged
- Ground-level release

At TMI, the core was severely damaged, but the containment held. The TMI release was very rapid at first, then tapered off.

Release Assessments: Chernobyl (1 of 3)

Next you will learn about what the Chernobyl accident taught us about conducting release assessments.

On April 26, 1986, an accident occurred at Unit 4 of the nuclear power station at Chernobyl, Ukraine, in the former USSR. The accident, caused by a sudden surge of power, destroyed the reactor and released massive amounts of radioactive material into the environment.

Release Assessments: Chernobyl (2 of 3)

On the first day of the accident, the release was 12 megacuries. For the next five days, the amount released decreased; then levels began to rise again.

Estimates of radionuclide released include: about 3–4% of the used fuel in the reactor at the time of the accident, 100% of noble gases and 20–60% of the volatile radionuclides were released. The radionuclide mix was complex. Iodine isotopes had the greatest short-term impact while cesium isotopes had the greatest long-term impact.

The food monitoring results from the Food and Drug Administration (FDA) and others following the Chernobyl accident support the conclusion that I-131, Cs-134, and Cs-137 are the principal radionuclides that contribute to radiation dose by ingestion following a nuclear reactor accident, but that Ru-103 and Ru-106 also should be included.

Release Assessments: Chernobyl (3 of 3)

The Chernobyl accident also provided some important historical data:
- The reactor failure resulted in an upward explosion (not a ground level release) causing dispersion over a very wide area. Much of the airborne radioactivity was driven into the stratosphere and upper atmosphere. This accounts for the relatively small number of deterministic health effects resulting from the accident.
- The mix of the release changed over time with wind direction.
- The plume was affected by the wind.
- Several hundred kilometers away, there were pockets of higher radiation from material deposited by rainout.

Next, you will learn about what the Fukushima incident taught us about conducting release assessments.

Release Assessments: Fukushima (1 of 2)

There have been no deaths or cases of radiation sickness resulting from the nuclear plant destruction precipitated by the regional disaster of March 11, 2011. However, as a result of the severe damage to station reactors and the subsequent radioactive material releases, more than 100,000 people were evacuated from their homes. Due to the dispersal of radioactive material across the regional environs, monitoring of the affected region, emergency workers, and members of the public will continue for many years.

The standard dose limit for radiation workers in Japan is 50 milli-sievert per year (mSv/yr) with a limit of 100 mSv over a 5-year period. As a result of the magnitude of this event, the emergency dose limit in Japan was raised to 250 mSv/year (25 rem/year) due to the seriousness of this accident. During the course of accident mitigation efforts, six workers received doses exceeding the emergency dose limit, one of these workers received a whole-body dose of 670 mSv and two workers received beta skin doses estimated at 2 to 3 Sv. 408 workers received doses in excess of the annual limit of 50 mSv.

Release Assessments: Fukushima (2 of 2)

Tokyo Electric Power Company (TEPCO) has estimated that the incident at Fukushima Daiichi resulted in the release of the following quantities of radioactive material:

- Noble gases – 500 PBq
- Iodine-131 – 500 PBq
- Cesium-137 – 10 PBq
- Cesium-134 – 10 PBq

About 20% of the radioactive material came from Unit 1 and about 40% each from Units 2 and 3. Major releases began on about March 15, three days after evacuation of the population out to 20 km. Much of the release was initially pushed over the ocean to the east of the station, but a significant quantity passed over and deposited on the ground to the west.

After Release

In the next section of the lesson you will learn about dose rates, deposition, and plume mixtures. In general, we know that after a release:

- Dose rates will be variable
- Deposition will be complex
- Mixture may vary
- Models do not make reliably accurate predictions

Most dose projection computer programs projection use straight-line Gaussian dispersion models. Mathematically, you can calculate a concentration of radioactive material downwind and off- centerline, and, therefore, a dose. The reality of environmental factors such as river valleys, terrain features, building wake, and crosswinds, however, often doesn't cooperate with mathematical formulas.

Whole-Body Dose and Plume Elevation

The projected whole-body dose at a location in the path of a release will vary depending upon whether the release is ground level or highly elevated. Elevation of the release can prevent high doses, as it did at Chernobyl, but cannot be predicted.

The side of the containment building is a likely failure point, leading to a ground level release. Even vented activity escaping through safety relief valves near buildings may be pulled down by building wake, effectively becoming a ground level release.

Plume Mixture (1 of 2)

The core damage state and timing of the release affects the mix of a release, causing the mixture in the plume to potentially change during the release.

Early in a release, normal coolant activity may be the only material released. As the accident progresses, gap activity (composed of other radioactive materials) may escape. Still later, as fuel melts, the composition of the release may change again.

Change in isotopic mixture in plume during release:
- Is different by core damage state.
- Can only make crude estimates.
- Can be confirmed by monitoring.
- Can change during release with wind direction.

Plume Mixture (2 of 2)

Often, a ratio of one radioisotope to a longer-lived radioisotope being released is used to differentiate release compositions. In the example shown in this image, strontium-89 is compared to cesium-137. During the gap release part of the incident depicted, no Sr-89 was released when the wind was blowing toward the northeast. However, when the wind shifted toward the northwest and the core melt release began, Sr-89 was evident. Later, when the wind shifted toward the southwest and vessel melt-through occurred, the ratio of Sr-89 to Cs-137 in the release increased significantly.

Deposition and Wind Shift

The actual dose for a major release can be elevated in any direction. For example, during the 1957 nuclear accident at Windscale, the following isotopes were released into the environment:
- 20,000 Ci of I-131
- 600 Ci of Cs-137
- 80 Ci of Sr-89
- 9 Ci of Sr-90

At TMI, the wind changed direction 360 degrees over 18 hours. Since a major release will most likely take place over several hours, wind shifts and high doses should be expected in several directions around the plant, not in a single direction. There is essentially no such thing as "downwind." The environment must be characterized (locate the deposited radioactive material).

Deposition Rate Variation with Surface, Location, and Time

Deposition rates following an accident will vary by surface, location, and time.

A significant part of the total dose to a population will be from deposited material.

Plume Direction (1 of 2)

Reasons why monitors at the plant may not record where the plume is going include:

- Diurnal heating and cooling at shorelines (lake effects)
- Local topographic obstacles
- Complex wind patterns

The list of reasons why monitors at the plant may not include where the plume is going continues on the next screen.

Plume Direction (2 of 2)

Additional reasons monitors at the plant may not record where the plume is going include:

- The wind moves in both horizontal and vertical planes and changes over the time of the release.
- If the monitor is placed in the line of the plume but the wind is moving upward, the monitor may not record the radiation from the plume at ground level. A single monitored measurement is insufficient to determine where a plume is going.
- The impact of release height will affect plume direction.

Experience and research have shown that the area affected by a reactor accident may be very large and complex (several states and/or countries). The public will demand proof of where contamination is and is not.

Lesson Summary

Let's summarize what you learned in this lesson:

- The greatest risk after an accident is to the population nearest the plant.
- It's difficult to predict which direction is actually downwind; monitor in all directions.
- Aerial and many ground-based monitoring teams will be needed.

In the next lesson you will learn about protective actions for reactor accidents and the emergency classification system.

Lesson 4: Protective Actions & Emergency Classification System

Lesson Overview

In this lesson you will learn about protective actions for reactor accidents and the emergency classification system.

Upon completion of this lesson, you will be able to:

- Describe accident classification and protective action decisions.

- Describe Nuclear Regulatory Commission (NRC) general emergency protective action guidance.

Remember you can access the glossary in one of two ways throughout this course. You can select the glossary button in the top right hand corner of each main content screen. In addition, on content screens you can select underlined words to access their definitions in the online glossary. Selecting an underlined word will take you directly to its definition in the glossary.

This lesson should take approximately **35 minutes** to complete.

Response Objectives

In the first section of this lesson, you will learn about protective actions that can be taken after reactor accidents. These are the emergency responses taken after an accident to reduce negative effects.

The objectives of emergency response after a reactor accident are to:
- Reduce the risk from or mitigate an accident at its source.
- Reduce the occurrence of severe deterministic health effects by keeping acute doses to critical organs below critical thresholds (50–100 rem).
- Take action to reduce cancer-producing effects.
- Do more good than harm in accordance with EPA/FDA guidelines.

Information Available at the Time of Event

At the time of the event, there is very little accurate information, but there may be a great deal of inaccurate information. Unfortunately, this is the time when the most important decisions need to be made.

Because of all the uncertainties involved, it is preferable to create a range to bound the possible consequences (consequences if the containment fails early, later, or not at all). Do not estimate conservatively or add conservatism just to be sure! The results will become meaningless and impossible to compare.

Information Provided to Decision Makers

Decision makers feel overwhelmed with information after an accident because the same information is being reported from different groups. Technical staff supporting the decision maker should:

- Provide known information (emergency class and core status).
- Try not to bias the decision maker.
- Give a best scientific estimate (not a conservative estimate).

There are priorities for decision makers following protective action guides (PAGs). Each of these priorities will now be covered in detail.

Priorities: Prevent Early Health Effects

The first priority after an accident is to prevent early health effects among the population in the path of the release.

Risks of Taking No Protective Action

By taking no protective action, an individual living near the plant has a 67% chance of exceeding 200 rem exposure.

Sheltering in a normal-frame home reduces the risk to 66%—virtually no reduction.

Even if the individual evacuates as the plume arrives, there is still a 55% probability of receiving a fatal dose of radiation.

Only evacuation before the plume arrives reduces the probability significantly, to 3%.

Research on Severe Accidents: Evacuation and Sheltering

Research on severe accidents tells us what actions we need to take and when we need to take them. The conclusion of past research shows:

- Core melt and early containment failures account for most of the risk of death off-site.
- Only evacuation before the release or shelter in a large building can substantially reduce the risk to those living within one mile of a plant where an accident occurs.
- Evacuation in plume does not increase the risk.

Why Wait to Evacuate?

To reduce the risk from a severe reactor accident, evacuation should be ordered early—before or shortly after a release.

Evacuation is much more effective than sheltering in reducing the potential for early deaths or health effects.

Urgent protective actions should be taken before or shortly after a release from a core damage accident.

Core damage can be predicted before a release, but the characteristics of a release cannot be predicted once the core has been damaged. Therefore, actions to be taken must be determined based on the status of the core.

Priorities: Reduce Stochastic Effects

As you learned earlier in this lesson, the first priority after an accident is to prevent early health effects among the population in the path of the release. The second priority after an accident is to reduce stochastic effects (cancers) from the release. In the next section of this lesson you will learn about stochastic effects.

Thyroid dose can be an important determinant of stochastic effects at great distances, via the ingestion pathway (i.e. consuming contaminated food such as milk). Many individuals who were children at the time of the Chernobyl accident and were exposed to released materials, even at great distances from the reactor itself, now have thyroid cancer.

Thyroid Blocking

Thyroid blocking is the process of preventing radioactive iodine from reaching the thyroid by first giving the individual large amounts of stable, nonradioactive iodine.

The stable iodine is most effective if taken 1 to 2 hours before the individual inhales the radioactive release.

If taken shortly after the individual inhales the radioactive release, it is still effective, but effectiveness drops rapidly to about 50% in 2 to 3 hours.

Chernobyl: Potassium Iodide Side Effects

18,000,000 single doses of potassium iodide (KI) were administered in Poland as a result of the Chernobyl accident. Though intended for children, doses were taken by some adults.

Out of all 18,000,000 doses administered, only two serious reactions were reported: both by adults who were allergic to iodine.

Based on this experience, there do not seem to be serious side effects from the use of KI as a prophylactic to reduce thyroid dose.

Protective Action Strategy

To reduce public risk for core damage accidents, officials should take the following protective action strategies:

- Evacuate or provide shelter within a two mile circle and five miles in the downwind sector and one sector on either side.
- Take thyroid blocking near the plant.
- Restrict consumption of locally grown food to at least 50 miles.
- Monitor to locate and evaluate hot spots in order to prevent severe deterministic health effects.
- Monitor to locate where food restrictions and relocation are warranted based on predetermined Derived Response Levels (DRLs).
- Revise the DRLs once the release mix is known.

Psychological Considerations

Psychological health effects should be expected after a nuclear accident. Past experience has shown that the effects are caused by a fear of radiation.

At Chernobyl, some actions taken by officials did more harm than good. Rural populations were relocated to cities, where the psychological impact of the accident, combined with the stress of relocation and higher crime and alcoholism rates, effectively reduced life expectancy.

Factors to Increase Public Trust

Trust in officials enhances popular compliance. Factors that build trust include:

- An ongoing information program
- Clear and simple advice during the accident

- Consistent advice and assessment (one official information point)

Emergency Classification System

Now that you have learned about protective actions you will learn about the system for defining which situations and accidents warrant prompt action, the emergency classification system.

Purpose of the Emergency Classification System

The emergency classification system for nuclear power plant accidents is designed to identify those accidents that warrant prompt action. It is the basis for fast, coordinated local, state and national action.

The nuclear power plant accident classification system is the basis for fast coordinated local, state, and national action for activation and notification, protective actions before a release, and notification of nearby states/counties if there is a potential of release.

The classification system is based on environmental monitoring and risks of core damage, judged by the critical safety system and barriers (core damage indication).

Accidents that Do Not Require Immediate Action to Protect the Public

Three classifications provide notification that something out of the ordinary is occurring:

- Notification of Unusual Event (NOUE) - The Notification of Unusual Event (NOUE) classification is the most commonly declared event. There is no threat to the fuel, no releases above technical specifications are expected, and there is usually no off-site response required.
- Alert - Events that impair plant safety are classified as Alerts. Off-site actions include notification, increased awareness, and ORO mobilization.
- Site Area Emergency (SAE) - At a Site Area Emergency (SAE), a potential for a release of radioactive material exists that might exceed EPA PAGs near the site boundary. Off-site response should include full mobilization, precautionary actions for special populations, and potential evacuation near site areas. In a General Emergency (GE), which will be covered on the next screen, protective actions for the public should be immediately implemented.

In these cases there is no need for immediate action to protect the public.

General Emergency (GE)

A General Emergency (GE) means that there is actual or projected severe core damage or that the operators have lost control of the plant. A GE warrants taking protective actions without any further discussions or meetings. The declaration of the emergency alone leads to protective actions being initiated. The reactor operator must also provide a protective action recommendation to off-site decision makers.

Frequency of General Emergencies

Statistically, the chances of a GE are between 1 in 5,000 and 1 in 10,000 per reactor year (RY).

The probability of a reactor accident is low; however, should such an accident occur, the consequences could be severe.

Reference Documents

Now that you have learned about protective actions and emergency classification, you will learn about reference documents with which you should be familiar. These include:

- The Nuclear Regulatory Commission's (NRC's) Response Technical Manual (RTM-96), used for accident assessment
- The NRC's Response Coordination Manual (RCM-96), used for accident coordination
- Criteria for Preparation and Evaluation of Radiological Emergency Response Plans and Preparedness in Support of Nuclear Power Plants (NUREG-0654/FEMA REP-1 rev.1)
- The Federal Radiological Monitoring and Assessment (FRMAC) Manuals

The next screens will provide more in depth information about each of these documents.

Response Technical Manual (RTM–96)

RTM-96 describes methods for assessing core damage and performing dose projections for those in the path of the release. The resulting estimates will help officials determine or confirm where to recommend protective actions for the public.

On the next few screens you will learn how RTM-96 includes information on the NRC's responsibilities, core damage assessment, classification, and protective action decision making.

RTM–96: NRC Responsibilities

The National Response Framework and the associated Nuclear/Radiological Incident Annex designates the NRC as a coordinating agency and as the lead technical agency. The NRC, because of its licensing authority, is the lead for an accident at a nuclear generating station. One of the first NRC on-site actions after such an accident is to begin assessing core damage.

On the next few screens you will learn how RTM-96 addresses core damage.

RTM-96: Core Damage Assessment

RTM-96 Section A outlines steps in assessing core damage. These steps include:

- Assessing the status of critical safety functions for indications that the core is uncovered
- Monitoring for indications that the core may soon become uncovered
- Projecting core damage if uncovered and informing decision makers
- Monitoring radiation levels to confirm and assess core damage
- Continue to assess core damage

Core damage assessment is a continual process. It should be conducted with the big picture in mind, and one instrument alone should never be used as the sole basis of a core assessment.

RTM-96: Condition Assessment Tool

RTM-96 is the NRC's principal tool for assessing core condition based on the amount of time the core was uncovered.

Other RTM-96 tables and charts show that containment monitor response is a key indicator of core damage.

NUREG-0654: Importance of Classification

Classification is the most important aspect in assessment of the accident in the early phase. Rapid classification and action, if necessary, is crucial. Classification as a GE will dictate immediate action and distinguish the accident from the other three possible classifications, none of which require immediate action. Unlike most exercise scenarios, GEs will possibly begin as GEs, requiring an immediate protective action for the public.

RTM-96: Protective Action Decision Making

RTM-96 includes a decision-making tool for determining protective actions necessary in the event of core damage or loss of control of the facility.

Response Coordination Manual (RCM-96)

In addition to RTM-96, you should also be familiar with RCM-96 which describes the types of interactions that may occur between the NRC and the other response organizations to provide an effective, coordinated response to a radiological emergency.

RCM-96 is a compilation of NRC documents that discusses various aspects of a response to an event at an NRC-licensed facility. The documents in RCM-96 focus primarily on non-technical coordination rather than technical analysis. Several documents that were previously published as NUREGs have been updated and are included.

Federal Radiological Monitoring and Assessment Center (FRMAC) Manuals

Other important reference documents with which you should be familiar are the FRMAC manuals. These are a multi-volume set of texts that provide a standard methodology for all activities associated with the FRMAC's environmental radiological monitoring, sampling, radioanalytical, and quality assurance programs.

These procedures are intended for use in responding to an emergency and processing relatively large numbers of samples in the shortest possible time.

The Department of Energy (DOE) has the responsibility for maintaining and revising the FRMAC manuals.

Lesson Summary

Let's summarize what you have learned in this lesson:

- Protective actions for reactor accidents take several priorities into consideration:
    - Preventing early health effects
    - Reducing stochastic effects
    - Following protective action strategy
    - Psychological effects
- The emergency classification system categorizes reactor accidents as: Notification of Unusual Event (NOUE)
    - Alerts

- Site Area Emergencies (SAE)
  - General Emergencies (GE)
- Several reference documents assist with monitoring and classifying reactor accidents:
  - RTM-96
  - RCM-96
  - NUREG-0654/FEMA REP-1 rev.1
  - FRMAC Manuals

The next lesson will cover the foundations of EPA Protective Action Guides, including units of dose, exposure pathways, and health effects.

Lesson 5: EPA PAGs – Dose, Exposure, and Effects

Lesson Overview

The purpose of this lesson is to introduce EPA Protective Action Guides (PAGs). This lesson also describes units of dose, exposure pathways, and health effects from exposure.

Upon completion of this lesson, you will be able to:

- Explain the purpose of the Environmental Protection Agency (EPA) Manual of Protective Action Guides and Protective Actions for Nuclear Incidents.
- Differentiate between total effective dose equivalent (TEDE), committed dose equivalent (CDE), committed effective dose equivalent (CEDE), and effective dose equivalent (EDE) in describing projected dose.
- Describe the radiation exposure pathways.
- Identify the health effects associated with each type of exposure.

Remember you can access the glossary in one of two ways throughout this course. You can select the glossary button in the top right hand corner of each main content screen. In addition, on content screens you can select underlined words to access their definitions in the online glossary.

This lesson should take approximately **1 hour** to complete.

Protective Actions and Protective Action Guides (PAGs)

As you learned in Lesson 1, the Environmental Protection Agency (EPA) has established protective action guides (PAGs) for the principal phases of a nuclear incident. The public usually can be protected in the case of a nuclear incident by some form of intervention that will disrupt normal living. Such intervention is called a protective action.

PAGs help public officials make protective decisions during a nuclear incident. Specifically, they outline the projected dose to a standard man (e.g., reference man) or other defined individual from an unplanned release of radioactive material, and the level at which a specific protective action to reduce or avoid that dose is warranted. They are primarily based on the avoidance of acute health effects.

EPA Protective Action Guides

The Environmental Protection Agency announced a revised manual titled Protective Action Guides And Planning Guidance For Nuclear Incidents (FR Vol. 78, No. 72, page 22258). This revised guidance is noticed for Interim Use and Public Comment and replaces the 1991 document when implemented. There is no ruling on when this new guidance must be implemented in State and local government plans and procedures. In the remainder of this course, the new guidance will be the basis for the lessons.

This lesson includes information concerning early phase (sometimes called the emergency or plume phase) and intermediate phase (also known as the post-plume phase) EPA protective action guides.

The PAG Manual is designed for the use of those in Federal, state, and local government with responsibility for emergency response planning and provides guidance for implementation of the protective actions.

Units of Dose

This lesson includes three major topics:

- Units of dose
- Exposure Pathways
- Health Effects

Let's begin by learning about units of dose.

Exposure (Roentgen) - Even though it is not a measure of dose, exposure needs to be discussed here as a related term in common use. Exposure measures the ability of photons (gamma and X-ray) to produce ionization in air. Most commonly available instruments give exposure rate in Roentgen per hour (R/hr) or milliRoentgen per hour (mR/hr). This quantity is useful in estimating the external hazard from radioactive material.

Absorbed Dose (rad and Gray) - Absorbed dose (rad) is a measure of energy imparted per unit mass. One rad is the dose delivered to any material that receives 100 ergs of energy per gram of that material.

The International System (SI) unit for absorbed dose is the Gray (Gy), which is the delivery of one joule per kilogram of material (100 rad = 1 Gray).

The rad (or Gy) is used to measure all ionizing radiation at any energy level. It does not, however, take into account the differing relative biological effectiveness (RBE) of different types of radiation. (The same dose of different types of radiation—alpha, beta, gamma—causes varying amounts of damage.) Therefore, to arrive at a calculated dose equivalent that represents biological damage, it is necessary to modify the absorbed dose by a modifying quality factor.

The modifying quality factors for varying radiations are as follows:
- X-ray, gamma, beta: 1
- Alpha, multicharged particles, fission fragments, heavy unknowns: 20
- Neutrons of unknown energy, high-energy protons: 10

- Neutrons based on energy (low to high): 2-11

Dose Equivalent (rem and Sievert) - The dose equivalent is a measure of biological damage that is calculated by multiplying absorbed dose by quality factor for the type of radiation involved.

The unit of dose equivalent is the rem. The SI unit is the Sievert (Sv). 100 rem = 1 Sv.

Dose equivalent quantities are calculated in dose projections; that is, they represent future dose calculated for a specified time period, in the absence of protective actions. They are then compared to PAGs for decisions on protective actions. Protective actions are taken to avoid projected dose.

Quantities of Projected Dose

Projected dose may be expressed in quantities of:
- Dose equivalent (DE)
- Effective dose equivalent (EDE)
- Committed dose equivalent (CDE)
- Committed effective dose equivalent (CEDE)
- Total effective dose equivalent (TEDE)

In the next section of this lesson, you'll learn more about each of these quantities.

Dose Equivalent (DE)

Dose equivalent (DE) is the product of the absorbed dose in organs/tissue (in rad or Gy) and modifying factors related to the relative biological effectiveness (RBE) of the radiation.

These factors are expressed in rem (or Sv). DE is usually used to express a dose to a particular organ.

For example:

1 rad of alpha delivered to lung tissue equals 20 rem DElung: 1 rad ? quality factor 20 (alpha) = 20 rem DElung.

Effective Dose Equivalent (EDE)

Effective dose equivalent (EDE) is the sum of the products of the DE to each organ and a weighting factor that is related to the risk of fatal cancer in the organs that have been exposed to the radiation. EDE is expressed in rem (or Sv). The weighting factors are as follows:
- Gonads – 0.25
- Breast – 0.15
- Red bone marrow – 0.12
- Thyroid – 0.03
- Bone surface 0.03
- Other organs – 0.30
- Whole body – 1.00

Suppose you wanted to determine the whole body risk of cancer caused by a 0.4 rem DE to the gonads. As the table on this screen demonstrates, the weighting factor for gonads is 0.25. A 0.4 rem gonadal dose x 0.25 = 0.1 rem EDE. The risk of a fatal cancer from a gonadal dose of 0.4 rem is about the same as that from a whole body dose of 0.1 rem.

The early-phase skin PAG for evacuation is 50 rem DE. The intermediate-phase beta skin PAG for relocation is 100 rem DE.

Committed Dose Equivalent (CDE)

Committed dose equivalent (CDE) measures the effect, over time, of radiation output from contaminants that have been internalized. It is the dose equivalent an organ or tissue will receive from intake during the 50-year period following the intake. The 50-year dose is dependent on:

- The physical characteristics of the isotope
- The chemical characteristics of the isotope
- Breathing rates
- Deposition velocities of the contaminant
- Pathways of internalization
- Biological removal mechanisms

For example, tritium (oxide) has a radiological half-life of 4.5 x 103 days (12.3 years). However, tritium has only a 12-day biological half-life, yielding also an effective half-life (combination of the two) of 12 days. Thus, most of the radiation dose resulting from tritium ingestion will be delivered in the first 12 days of the 50-year calculated period.

The early-phase thyroid PAG for evacuation is 5 rem CDE.

Committed Effective Dose Equivalent (CEDE)

Committed effective dose equivalent (CEDE) is the total internal dose the body receives in the 50 years after the inhalation or ingestion of radioactive materials with respect to the risk of fatal cancer in the affected organs. It is calculated by:

- Multiplying, for each tissue or organ irradiated, the weighting factor applicable to that tissue or organ by the CDE to that organ, then
- Adding together the results obtained for each individual organ.

For example, suppose the thyroid received a CDE of 25 rem from an I-131 uptake. Suppose further that the thyroid also received a CDE of 5 rem from an I-132 uptake. The weighting factor for the thyroid is 0.03; therefore, the CEDE is 0.90 rem.

[(25 x 0.03) + (5 x 0.03) = 0.90].

Total Effective Dose Equivalent (TEDE)

Total effective dose equivalent (TEDE) is a Nuclear Regulatory Commission (NRC) term that combines the effects of both the internal and external exposures. It is the sum of the deep dose equivalent (DDE), dose to the skin to a depth of 1 cm, from external gamma radiation and the CEDE from internal exposure. The term TEDE is not used in the current PAG Manual but will be used in any revisions of the manual that may be issued. For our purposes, DDE and EDE are synonymous.

For example, suppose exposure to a concentration of 1 x 10–6 µCi/cc of I-131 for 1 hour yielded a 1.3 rem CDEthyroid dose. 1.3 rem CDEthyroid x 0.03 weighting factor (for thyroid) = 0.039 rem CEDE. That same concentration yielded an external dose of 0.014 rem EDE. Therefore, the TEDE dose received was 0.053 rem (TEDE = EDE + CEDE).

The early-phase TEDE evacuation PAG is 1 rem.

The intermediate-phase TEDE relocation PAG is 2 rem (1st year).

Exposure Pathways

Now that you have learned about units of dose, you will learn about the pathways through which people can be exposed to radiation.

Radiation Exposure Pathways (1 of 2)

During and after a release of radioactive material, individuals may be exposed to radiation through a variety of pathways. Pathways that contribute less than 10% of the total dose need not be considered in determining the potential dose for purposes of comparing it to the PAG.

Major and minor exposure pathways considered in developing the EPA and FDA PAGs include:
- Plume shine
- Immersion in the plume
- Deposited materials
- Resuspended materials
- External contamination
- Ingestion of contaminated food and water

Radiation Exposure Pathways (2 of 2)

Some of these pathways apply only to the early phase, others only to the intermediate phase, and some to both phases.

For example, the following are included in dose projections for early-phase evacuation PAGs:

- Plume shine
- Immersion in the plume
- Deposited materials

Included in calculations for intermediate-phase relocation PAGs are:

- Resuspended materials
- External contamination

Planning must take into account dealing with members of the public and emergency responders who become externally contaminated with radioactive material. Ingestion of contaminated food and water is considered in FDA ingestion PAGs, and will be covered in Lesson 9.

You will learn more about each of these pathways in the next section of this lesson.

Plume Shine

An airborne plume may contain:

- The noble gases (xenon and krypton, which emit both beta and gamma radiation).
- Radioiodines (also beta and gamma emitters).
- Various radioactive particulates.

For those in the path of a plume, exposure to gamma radiation from the airborne radioactive materials overhead called plume shine (sometimes called cloudshine or sky shine) is the leading exposure pathway and contributes to external dose. Since the plume may be a considerable distance away from or above the population affected, the gamma components are the only contributors of exposure (the beta components present a negligible threat). This exposure ends when the plume is gone.

Immersion in the Plume (1 of 3)

Immersion is the state of being completely surrounded by a radioactive plume. It leads to:

- External exposure to both beta and gamma radiation.
- External contamination from radionuclides in the plume.
- Internal exposure and contamination due to inhalation.

Because of the nearness of the radioactive material, those immersed in a plume are externally exposed to both beta and gamma radiation.

Immersion in the Plume (2 of 3)

Inhalation of radioiodines has the potential to result in large doses to the thyroid in certain nuclear power plant accidents.

Radioiodines:

- Are present in large numbers because a large inventory is created during fission and is available for release.
- Are absorbed through lung tissue and circulate through the body via the bloodstream.
- Will concentrate in the thyroid gland, producing a specific organ dose (CDE).

Those leaving the plume must be monitored and decontaminated to end their external exposure. Medical evaluation and treatment may be necessary to reduce their internal exposure.

Immersion in the Plume (3 of 3)

Protecting the thyroid from radioiodine can be accomplished by:

- Evacuation prior to arrival of the plume containing radioiodine.
- Respiratory protection, though usually limited to on-site emergency workers during specific situations.
- Administration (ingestion) of potassium iodide (KI), though it may not be available to the public.

Exposure to particulates, such as cesium and strontium, can lead to a major internal dose if such particulates are released from containment. The dose due to inhalation of Cs-137 while being exposed to a concentration of 1 μCi/cc for 1 hour is 3.8 x 104 rem committed effective dose equivalent.

Inhalation of noble gases is not considered an inhalation hazard because:

- Noble gases are inhaled and then exhaled.
- They are chemically inert (group VIII of the Periodic Table). They are, however, still radioactive and yield an external dose.

Deposited Materials (1 of 2)

External exposure to beta and gamma radiation from materials deposited on the ground is sometimes called groundshine. However, the beta component is not expected to be a controlling factor in determining whether an evacuation is required during a nuclear reactor accident.

Soon after a release, there may be doses to the public from both airborne and deposited radioactive materials. Since the deposition dose to persons not evacuated will continue until they are relocated, evacuation PAG dose calculations assume four days of exposure. The four-day exposure assumption is based on the duration of the primary release being less than four days, and the exposure to deposited materials after four days being addressed through protective actions such as relocation, if warranted. Four days of gamma exposure from the deposited radionuclides could be a significant contributor to total dose received during the early phase, especially if the release contains large quantities of radioiodines or particulates.

Deposited Materials (2 of 2)

Intermediate-phase relocation PAGs involve calculations of gamma exposure from deposition for the first year after termination of a release. Long-term goals include two-year and fifty-year exposure calculations.

The PAG Manual states on page 45, "For situations where it is impractical to meet these objectives though decontamination, consideration should be given to relocation at a lower projected first year dose than that specified by the relocation PAG."

Resuspended Materials

Calculations show that in reactor accidents, the dose from inhalation of resuspended materials is usually not an exposure pathway controlling the decision to relocate during the early or intermediate phases. Resuspension factors will vary between site locations. Verification of resuspension factors for a given site is therefore necessary. This is accomplished by air sampling.

A resuspension factor of 1 x 10-6 has been demonstrated, for example, for non-arid locations. Thus, if one curie of a material has been deposited per square meter in a non-arid location, typically only one microCurie (1 x 10-6 Ci) per cubic meter will be in the air above the ground.

External Contamination (1 of 2)

If an area has been contaminated by the passing plume, the potential exists for people to be contaminated and/or receive dose from passing through it. Beta and gamma exposure will continue for the contaminated individuals after they leave the area until they are decontaminated.

External Contamination (2 of 2)

External beta exposure pathways include:

- Direct exposure from immersion in the plume
- Exposure from materials deposited on skin and clothing
- Exposure from materials deposited on nearby surfaces

Beta exposure is not expected to be the controlling factor in determining protective actions required for reactor accidents. Evacuation is not the preferred protective action for external beta exposure. Showering and changing clothes will reduce or eliminate external contamination on individuals. Evacuation, however, is warranted for protection from an associated high inhalation dose.

External beta PAGs are 50 times higher than gamma PAGs.

Health Effects of Radiation

Now that you have learned about units of dose and the pathways through which individuals can be exposed, you will learn about the health effects of radiation.

Radiation Health Effects

The dose from exposure to radioactive material may be delivered only during the period of environmental exposure (e.g., external gamma radiation), or over a longer period (e.g., inhaled radionuclides that are deposited in organs). In the latter case, the dose not only is delivered at the time of intake from the environment but also continues until all of the radioactive material has decayed or been eliminated from the body.

The health effects of radiation include:

- Acute health effects
- Brain damage to the unborn
- Delayed health effects Radiogenic cancers
- Thyroid disorders and cancers
- Genetic disorders

The risk of acute health effects is the primary basis for setting EPA PAG values. Avoidance of health effects from accidents that involve the release of radioactive materials is the primary justification for all radiological emergency planning.

On the following screens, you will learn about these types of health effects.

Acute Health Effects (1 of 2)

Three factors define acute health effects:

- Prompt radiation effects (observable within a short time period, two to three months after exposure)
- Varying severity of effect, depending on dose
- Existence of a practical threshold

PAG values and emergency worker dose limits are set low enough to avoid these effects.

Acute Health Effects (2 of 2)

EPA's PAG Manual further describes acute effects as either severe or non-severe.

Severe effects (including death) occur at high doses and have clinically observable symptoms. Prodromal effects (first indicators of damage) are not severe in themselves but are a forewarning of more severe effects.

Prodromal effects include:
- Anorexia (loss of appetite)
- Nausea
- Vomiting
- Diarrhea
- Epilation (hair loss)
- Erythema (skin reddening)
- Fatigue
- Nonmalignant skin damage

Non-severe effects include hematological deficiencies, temporary infertility, and chromosomal changes. These may not be considered severe, but are detrimental to the individual's health in varying degrees.

Brain Damage to the Unborn

Brain damage to the unborn is a class of injury reported in atomic bomb survivors that does not fall into either an acute or delayed effect category, but exhibits elements of both.

Radiation doses received in the eighth to fifteenth weeks of gestation pose the greatest risk to the fetus. Potential health effects include:
- Small head (microcephaly)
- Small brain (microencephaly)
- Mental retardation

The risk per unit dose during this period in a pregnancy is taken to be about 4 x 10-3 per rad of dose. Because of this relatively high risk, special consideration should be given to the protection of the fetus during this period. The National Council on Radiation Protection (NCRP) has recommended an exposure limit of 0.5 rem for pregnant women.

Delayed Health Effects

Now that you've learned about acute health effects and brain damage to the unborn, you will now learn about delayed health effects considered in establishing PAGs.

The risk of delayed health effects in exposed individuals is the second principle involved in establishing PAGs.

According to the PAGs, the risk of delayed effects (primarily cancer and genetic effects, which are assumed to have linear non-threshold relationships to dose) should not exceed upper bounds that are judged to be adequately protective of public health under emergency conditions, and are reasonably achievable.

Delayed Health Effects: Cancer

Radiogenic cancers are stochastic effects. That is, the chance of getting cancer is proportional to the dose received, but the severity is not proportional to the dose received (e.g., you either get or don't get cancer).

There may be no threshold dose. There is a latent period associated with the onset of radiation-induced cancers, so the increased risk due to exposure to radiation is not immediately apparent.

The increased risk is assumed to commence two to ten years after the time of exposure and continue the remainder of the exposed individual's lifespan. Risk data are based on studies of Japanese A-bomb survivors, but risk estimates continue to change.

Delayed Health Effects: Thyroid Cancer

Thyroid exposure to very high levels of radiation may cause degeneration of the thyroid. At moderate levels of exposure some loss of thyroid function will occur. At lower levels, there are delayed health effects, which take the form of both thyroid nodules and thyroid malignancies. Doses as low as 14 rad to the thyroid have been associated with thyroid malignancy.

In adults, the increased risk of radiation-induced cancer is assumed to commence about 10 years after initial exposure and continue for the remaining lifespan of the exposed individual. The early-phase evacuation PAG is 5 rem CDE to the thyroid.

Delayed Health Effects: Skin Cancer

The risk of fatal skin cancer is estimated to be on the order of 1% of the total risk of fatal cancer for uniform irradiation of the entire body.

The ratio of nonfatal to fatal skin cancers from irradiation of the skin is high (100 to 1).

The early-phase evacuation PAG is 50 rem EDE to the skin.

Delayed Health Effects: Fetal Cancers

A fetus is estimated to be five to ten times as sensitive to radiogenic cancer as an adult.

There are reports of increased relative incidence of childhood cancers following prenatal X-ray doses as low as 0.20–0.25 rem and of doubling of childhood cancers following prenatal X-ray doses between 1 and 4 rem.

Delayed Health Effects: Genetic Disorders

An average parental dose of 1 rem before a baby's conception has been estimated to produce between 5 and 75 significant genetically related disorders per million liveborn offspring. Taking into account all genetically related disorders, the estimated risk of genetically related disorders in all generations is 1×10^{-4} per person-rem (collective dose of all those exposed) to a typical population.

Estimates of all radiation-induced genetic effects include:

- 50%: Minor to moderate medical problems
- 25%: Severe medical problems
- 23%: Require extended hospitalization
- 2%: Die before age 20

Lesson Summary

- Let's summarize what you have learned in this lesson:
    - Projected dose may be expressed in quantities of:
    - Dose equivalent (DE) Effective dose equivalent (EDE)
    - Committed dose equivalent (CDE)
    - Committed effective dose equivalent (CEDE)
    - Total effective dose equivalent (TEDE)
- Pathways considered in developing the EPA and FDA PAGs include: Plume shine
    - Immersion in the plume
    - Deposited materials
    - Resuspended materials
    - External contamination
    - Ingestion of contaminated food and water
- The health effects of radiation include:
    - Acute health effects
    - Brain damage to the unborn
    - Delayed health effects

The next lesson will cover the implementation guidance in the EPA PAG Manual.

Lesson 6: EPA PAGs – EPA PAGs – Implementation Guidance

Lesson Overview

As you learned in Lesson 1, during a nuclear incident when the source of exposure to the public is not under control, the public usually can be protected only by some form of intervention that will disrupt normal living. Such an intervention is termed a protective action. This lesson covers the guidelines included in the EPA PAG Manual.

Upon completion of this lesson, you will be able to:

- Explain the purpose of protective action guides (PAGs).
- Describe the importance of incident phases in planning for emergency response.
- Identify protective actions for the early and intermediate phases of a radiological incident.

Remember you can access the glossary in one of two ways throughout this course. You can select the glossary button in the top right hand corner of each main content screen. In addition, on content screens you can select underlined words to access their definitions in the online glossary. Selecting an underlined word will take you directly to its definition in the glossary.

This lesson should take approximately **30 minutes** to complete.

EPA Protective Action Guides

A Protective Action Guide (PAG) is a decision level for public officials during a nuclear incident. More specifically, it is the projected radiation dose to a standard individual, or other defined individual, from an unplanned release of radioactive material at which a specific protective action to reduce or avoid that dose is warranted. Projected radiation dose is the dose estimated to be received in a specified time in the absence of protective actions.

The EPA PAGs apply to all nuclear incidents or accidents except nuclear war. Nuclear incident or accident sites include:

- Nuclear power plants
- Other nuclear facilities (fuel cycle, defense and research, producers or users or radioisotopes)
- Nuclear weapons (nondetonation)
- Transportation
- Satellites (launch or reentry)
- Radiological dispersion devices (RDD)
- Improvised nuclear devices (IND)

A nuclear incident is defined as an event or a series of events, either deliberate or accidental, leading to a release, or potential release, into the environment of radioactive material in sufficient quantity to warrant consideration of protective actions.

Applicability of EPA PAGs

PAGs apply equally to almost all population groups. Exceptions apply in high-risk situations and for some special populations. Examples of these exceptions include:

- Presence of severe weather
- Competing disasters, such as a chemical spill
- Institutionalized persons who are not readily mobile (critical care patients, inmates, etc.)
- Local physical factors that impede evacuation

Nuclear Incident Phases

It is generally accepted that all nuclear incident sequences pass through three common phases; within each phase, different considerations apply to most protective actions. These common phases include:

- **Early** - At the beginning of a nuclear incident involving a large release of radioactive material to the atmosphere, when immediate decisions for effective use of protective actions are required. This phase is also called plume or emergency phase. Doses may accrue in this phase from airborne and deposited radioactive material as well as from inhalation of radionuclides.

- **Intermediate** - Beginning after the source and releases have been brought under control and reliable environmental measurements are available. Doses may accrue in this phase from deposited, resuspended, and ingested radioactive material.
- **Late**- Beginning when actions are commenced to reduce radiation levels in the environment to acceptable levels to allow inhabitants unrestricted use of the area. This phase is also referred to as the recovery phase. Currently, there are no EPA PAGs specific to the late phase.

It is important to note that PAGs have been developed for the first two phases of a nuclear accident: early and intermediate.

Now that you've learned about the common phases of nuclear incidents, let's examine how PAGs are designed to be used for planning purposes.

Planning (1 of 2)

PAGs are designed to be used for planning purposes, for example, to develop radiological emergency response plans and to exercise those plans. They provide guidance for response decisions and should not be regarded as dose limits.

The phase sequence described on the previous screen is most useful for planning. Different types of protective actions are required in each of the phases. The PAG for each phase has been constructed independent of the PAG for the other phases. For the purpose of working with the PAGs, any dose received during the early phase is not subtracted from a projected dose during the intermediate phase.

Another way of thinking of this would be that doses are not additive from phase to phase. PAG doses are based on avoidable dose and doses which have already been received are not included in subsequent decisions.

Planning (2 of 2)

Conditions and characteristics that are unique to each phase can affect the planning during an incident. Select the links to learn more about planning considerations during each phase.

- **During early phase –**
  - The release is still ongoing
  - Evacuation may be necessary because of potential exposure to external radiation from immersion in the plume
  - Potential exposure pathways are cloudshine, groundshine, and immersion
- **During intermediate phase –**
  - There is no chance of further release
  - The plume has dissipated
  - Environmental data collection activities should have begun
  - Food and water controls may have been instituted
  - Resuspension of radioactive materials and deposited radionuclides may require relocation and decontamination of surfaces
- **During late phase –**

- o Decontamination down to an established exposure rate or concentration may be necessary before an area can be reused

PAGs as Decision Levels

PAGs are decision levels for public officials. They are used to determine actions that will minimize risk from an event that is occurring or has already occurred.

The decision to advise members of the public to take an action to protect themselves from radiation from a nuclear incident involves a complex judgment in which the risk avoided by the protective action must be weighed in the context of the risks involved in taking the action.

Furthermore, the decision may have to be made under emergency conditions, with little or no detailed information available. Therefore, considerable planning is necessary to reduce to a manageable level the complexity of decisions required to effectively protect the public at the time of an incident.

Mandatory for Planning

Effective planning for nuclear incidents includes developing radiological emergency response plans. PAGs provide guidance for response decisions and should not be regarded as dose limits. Because conditions during a real incident cannot be anticipated when guidelines are developed during planning, professional judgment will be required in applying response plans to actual incidents.

The incident phases are independent from each other; however, they may overlap in terms of the potential exposure pathways involved and the protected actions required.

Resources used in the early phase may continue to be used in the intermediate phase. Dose limits for workers, however, are different for the first two phases. For the purposes of PAGs, doses accrued in the early phase are considered independently of those accrued in the intermediate.

PAG Supplemental Radiation Protection

The main contributors to radiation protection at fixed facilities are:
- Site selection
- Plant design
- Quality assurance in plant construction
- Engineered safety systems
- Competence of staff in safe operation and maintenance

These measures can reduce both the probability and magnitude of potential consequences of an accident.

Risks and Rewards of PAGs

PAGs are designed to protect all individuals in the population. However, some protective measures themselves present a certain degree of risk, and some population groups are at different levels of risk from those protective measures. The risk from being exposed must exceed the risk of implementing the protective action recommended.

Next you will learn about the protective actions and how they apply to the phases of radiological incidents.

Protective Actions

Protective actions are activities conducted in response to an incident or potential incident to avoid or reduce radiation dose to members of the public. Protective actions are sometimes called protective measures.

Early phase protective actions - Evacuation and sheltering (supplemented by bathing and changes of clothing) are the principal protective actions for use during the early phase to protect the public from exposure to direct radiation and inhalation from an airborne plume. It may be appropriate to initiate protective actions for the milk supply, and if included in emergency plans, to issue KI to reduce thyroid dose.

Intermediate phase protective actions - There are two types of protective actions during the intermediate phase. Relocation and decontamination are the principal protective actions taken to protect the public from whole-body external exposure due to deposited material and from inhalation of any resuspended radioactive particulates during the intermediate and late phases. The second type of protective action encompasses restrictions on the consumption and use of contaminated food and water. These protective actions will be discussed in the Lesson 9. During the intermediate phase of an incident, a new set of PAGs is used to determine the need to relocate from an area where contamination levels would cause an individual's dose to exceed 2 rem TEDE in the first year following the cessation of the release. Long-term goals include relocation of individuals if the second-year, or any subsequent year, TEDE dose would exceed 0.5 rem, and 50-year dose would exceed 5 rem TEDE.The PAG Manual states on page 4-4, "For situations where it is impractical to meet these objectives though decontamination, consideration should be given to relocation at a lower projected first year dose than that specified by the relocation PAG." In the intermediate phase, protective actions are based on environmental measurements.

Some protective actions are not addressed by assignment of a PAG (e.g., access control and ad hoc respiratory protection). Access control is instituted during the first two phases to prevent individuals from exposing themselves unnecessarily by entering an area affected by the radioactive material. Respiratory protection is usually applicable for supplementary protection in some circumstances, usually by emergency workers.

Precautionary Actions

Precautionary actions are not defined or discussed explicitly in the PAG Manual. However, in the FEMA REP Program Manual (June 2013), precautionary protective actions are defined as any preventive or emergency protective actions implemented without the verification of radionuclide measurements by field monitoring or laboratory analysis.

Evacuation

The EPA defines evacuation as the urgent removal of people to avoid or reduce high-level, acute exposure from a plume and/or deposited radioactive materials.

How is evacuation different from relocation?

- Evacuation is the primary protective action to prevent dose from the airborne plume.
- Relocation, which will be discussed later in this lesson, is used in the intermediate phase rather than in the early phase. Relocation is the removal or continued exclusion of people (households) from contaminated areas to avoid low-level, long-term chronic radiation exposure.

Evacuation: Basis for Decision

The decision to evacuate is based on:

- Plant conditions: whether the potential exists for doses to exceed PAGs beyond the site boundary.
- Projected dose: based on predicted, potential, or actual releases. Environmental measurements should be collected to verify whether the initial designated area for evacuation included all areas that exceeded the PAGs.

Evacuation: Considerations

The 1975 EPA study "Evacuation Risks—An Evaluation" concluded that:

- Evacuation provides complete protection from radiation if implemented before the plume arrives.
- Risks associated with automobile travel in contaminated areas are known.
- Risk of injury or death from automobile travel does not change during an evacuation.
- The risk from evacuation was considered in establishing the PAG.

Evacuation Summary

- Sheltering may be preferable to evacuation in some situations, but usually only if environmental constraints, such as competing disasters (e.g., debris after tornado has blocked roads), exist.
- People can be evacuated from affected areas with minimal risk.
- Neither panic nor hysteria is typically observed when evacuations of large areas are managed by public officials.
- Most evacuees use their own transportation and provide their own food and shelter.
- Advance planning and exercising are essential to identifying potential problems that may occur in an evacuation.

Sheltering

FEMA and the Nuclear Regulatory Commission (NRC) define sheltering-in-place as going inside, closing all doors, turning off heat and air conditioning systems and tuning radio or TV to an emergency station. The most protective areas in the home are a central area or the basement.

Sheltering effectiveness is significantly reduced if windows or doors are opened or large cracks are present. Risk of failure of sheltering is assumed to be high. Sheltering is usually not appropriate in areas where high doses are projected or where exposure might last longer than two complete air exchanges of the shelter.

Potassium Iodide (KI)

Another protective action that might be taken concurrent with or after an exposure event is the administration of potassium iodide (KI).

Administration of stable KI blocks inhaled radioiodine from accumulating in the thyroid gland. KI should not be used as an alternative to evacuation if evacuation prior to exposure is feasible.

You will learn more about KI dosage in Lesson 8.

Potassium Iodide (KI): Effectiveness

KI protects only the thyroid from inhaled or ingested radioiodine.

- KI is 95% effective in blocking thyroid absorption of radioiodine when taken one to two hours before or concurrently with exposure.
- KI is 50% effective when taken three to four hours after exposure.
- KI is minimally effective when taken 12 hours after exposure.
- KI is 50% effective when taken 30 to 50 hours before intake of radioiodine.

Potassium Iodide: Side Effects

The risk of incidence and the severity of side effects from KI are uncertain. However, the FDA has stated that the risk of thyroid nodules and cancer from 25 rem to the thyroid outweighs the risk of side effects from KI administration.

KI is contraindicated for persons with known allergies to iodine. Medical procedures for iodine allergy testing are available, and approval by medical officials for KI ingestion is advised for all persons before taking KI.

FEMA recommends distribution of KI to emergency workers and institutionalized persons and if the state approves, the public, for use during emergencies. You will learn more about the administration of KI in Lesson 8.

Relocation

Relocation is the removal or continued exclusion of people from contaminated areas to avoid chronic exposure to radiation leading to a dose exceeding the intermediate-phase relocation PAG of:

- 2 rem TEDE or 100 rem DE skin beta in the 1st year
- 0.5 rem TEDE 2nd or subsequent years

Individuals already evacuated may be converted to relocated status if their residence or place of employment is located in the area that exceeds the relocation PAG. Personnel not evacuated during the early phase may now require relocation.

Evacuees may return to areas not within the restricted zone (RZ). Those who must reenter the RZ for important duties must use radiation protection methods.

Relocation: Constraints

For relocation to be recommended, the following exposure rates must be calculated at 1 meter from the ground that equates to:

- 2 rem TEDE in the first year
- 0.5 rem TEDE in the second or subsequent years

Determination of areas to be restricted should be based on factors such as:

- The mix of radionuclides in deposited materials
- Calculated exposure rates versus the PAGs
- Field samples of vegetation and soil analysis

The boundary of the RZ must be established and all within that boundary are candidates for relocation. The easiest method entails using aircraft with sensitive radiation detection equipment capable of correcting the readings to one meter from the ground.

Access Control

The purpose of access control is to restrict access to the affected area. It supplements protection from sheltering, evacuation, and relocation. There is no PAG for access control.

The advantage of access control is that is provides a simple and effective way of reducing risk to people outside the affected area.

There are also constraints on access control. Effective communications and traffic control are required to implement access control effectively. Planning is necessary to ensure the presence of sufficient resources to adequately control the access. Access control may be a long-term undertaking.

Control of Surface Contamination

If aerosols or particulate materials are released during an incident, the resulting plume can be expected to deposit radioactive materials on the areas over which it passes. In extreme cases, individuals and equipment may be highly contaminated, and screening stations will be required for emergency monitoring and decontamination of individuals and for determining which individuals need medical evaluation. Equipment should be checked at this point and decontaminated as necessary to avoid the spread of contamination to other locations.

Once the RZ boundary has been established, in the intermediate phase, emergency personnel may reenter the RZ under controlled conditions in accordance with occupational dose limit criteria. Monitoring stations will be required at locations near the RZ boundary. Because of the potential high background radiation at these gross monitoring stations, significant amounts of contamination may be undetectable.

Additional monitoring stations may be needed at nearby low-background areas.

Decontamination (1 of 2)

Decontamination involves the removal of radioactive material from surfaces. Washing and changing clothing is recommended primarily to provide protection from beta radiation from radioiodines and particulate materials deposited on the skin or clothing. During the emergency, there is no need to control the runoff from personnel decontamination efforts. During the emergency phase, monitoring and decontamination efforts may take place a considerable distance from the affected area.

Urgent medical care should not be delayed for decontamination efforts or for time-consuming protection of attendants. Monitoring and decontamination also should not be allowed to delay evacuation from high- or potentially high-exposure-rate areas.

Select this link to access a table that describes the recommended surface contamination screening levels for emergency screening of persons and other surfaces at screening or monitoring stations in high background radiation areas.

Decontamination (2 of 2)

After the RZ is established, it may be necessary to move monitoring and decontamination facilities to locations near the boundary of the RZ.

Because background levels may be higher near the RZ, low levels of contamination may be undetectable. Individuals exiting the RZ found to be uncontaminated nevertheless should be advised to bathe and change clothes within the next 24 hours.

Lesson Summary

Let's summarize what you learned in this lesson:

- A protective action guide (PAG) is a projected dose at which actions to reduce or avoid that dose is warranted.
- Nuclear incidents generally pass through three common phases; early, intermediate, and late phases.
- Precautionary action is an action taken on the basis of the potential for a release of radioactive material.
- Evacuation, sheltering, and administration of potassium iodide are some of the protective actions that should be taken in the early phases of an incident.
- Relocation is a protective action that should be taken in the intermediate phase of an incident.

Lesson 7: EPA PAGs – Emergency Worker Dose Limits

Lesson Overview

In this lesson you will learn about recommendations for protecting emergency workers in the event of a nuclear incident or accident.

Upon completion of this lesson, you will be able to:

- List categories of emergency workers and define special circumstances where higher dose limits for emergency workers may be appropriate.
- Differentiate between emergency worker limits, occupational worker limits, and protective action guides (PAGs).
- Summarize recommendations for emergency worker protection described in the EPA PAG Manual.
- Identify methods of managing and monitoring internal exposure during the early phase.

Remember you can access the glossary in one of two ways throughout this course. You can select the glossary button in the top right hand corner of each main content screen. In addition, on content screens you can select underlined words to access their definitions in the online glossary. Selecting an underlined word will take you directly to its definition in the glossary.

This lesson should take approximately **20 minutes** to complete.

Emergency Worker Categories

State and local authorities designate what categories of workers are classified as emergency workers. The PAG Manual is careful to delegate the decision on what constitutes an emergency worker to state and local authorities. Examples of categories that may be designated as emergency workers include:

- Law Enforcement
- Firefighters
- Radiation Protection
- Civil Defense
- Emergency Management Traffic Control
- Health Services
- Transportation Services
- Animal Care

In addition, select workers at institutions, utilities, industrial facilities, farms as well as other agriculture-based businesses may be designated as emergency workers.

Dose Limits

Emergency worker dose limits and protective action guides (PAGs) are not the same. PAGs are not limits; they are projected doses that warrant taking a protective action. PAGs consider the risks to individuals from exposure to radiation, and the risks and costs associated with a specific protective action. The risk involved in taking a protective action should not exceed the radiation risk incurred if the protective action is not taken.

Emergency worker dose limits are based on a federally acceptable level of risk of health effects and may be adjusted based on the collective dose to the population being protected.

Any resulting exposures will be considered justified if the maximum risks permitted to workers are acceptably low by Federal standards and the risks or costs to others that are avoided by the workers' actions outweigh the risks to which the workers are subjected.

Emergency Worker Dose Limits in the Early Phase (1 of 3)

Emergency worker dose limits include all doses received during the early phase. PAGs consider a future dose that may be avoided. Emergency workers may also use protective equipment, protective clothing, and dosimetry to monitor their dose. You will learn more about these methods later in this lesson.

Occupational guidance specifies that:

- Doses to workers should be maintained as low as reasonably achievable (ALARA).
- Doses should be monitored.
- Workers should be informed of the risks involved and of the basic principles for radiation protection.

Higher dose limits for workers are allowed when required to:

- Prevent substantial risks to populations.
- Protect valuable property.
- Save lives.

Emergency Worker Dose Limits in the Early Phase (2 of 3)

When accessing this table, keep in mind the following key points:

- The dose limit in this table is the TEDE.
- Dose to the eye lens should be limited to three times the listed value.
- Dose to any other organ (including skin and body extremities) should be limited to 10 times the listed value.
- There was a separate CDE thyroid dose limit of 25 rem. FDA previously recommended thyroid blocking to those who were likely to receive a projected dose of 25 rem to the thyroid. The current recommendation is 130 mg for non-pregnant adults between 18 and 40 at 10 rem, and 130 mg for those over 40 at 500 rem.
- Emergency worker limits apply during the duration of the emergency. No specific guidance is given on when the emergency ends, but it is usually considered to be when the release has terminated, the public has been evacuated, and valuable property has been protected from fires, etc.

Emergency Worker Dose Limits in the Early Phase (3 of 3)

Doses received as emergency workers or from living in a slightly contaminated area are considered "once in a lifetime" doses and are not additive for the purpose of occupational exposure records. It is logical for occupational workers to add doses received as emergency workers to records as "planned special exposures."

Minors and pregnant women should not be designated as emergency workers. Their dose should not exceed 0.5 rem.

The Federal Radiological Protection Coordinating Committee (FRPCC) PAG subcommittee has decided to issue no additional guidance to the states on how to implement emergency worker dose limits. States are expected to:

- Work out the details in their plans.
- Include procedures in their plans for managing dose to emergency workers.

Emergency Worker Dose Limits in the Intermediate Phase

Individuals who are permitted to reenter the restricted zone (RZ) to work or for other justified reasons will require protection from radiation. Such individuals should enter the RZ under controlled conditions in accordance with dose limitations and other procedures for control of occupationally exposed workers.

Ongoing doses received by these individuals from living in a contaminated area outside the RZ need not be included as part of this dose limitation. In addition, dose received previously during the emergency phase need not be considered as part of the intermediate-phase limits.

Occupational dose limits per year are as follows:

- TEDE: 5 rem
- CDE (eye): 15 rem
- DE (shallow, skin and extremity): 50 rem
- DDE + CDE (other than eye): 50 rem

Dose to minors must be limited to 10% of the above limits. Dose to pregnant females is limited to 500 mrem TEDE per entire nine-month period and no substantial variation above a uniform monthly rate.

Managing and Monitoring Internal Exposure During the Early Phase

Now that you have learned about emergency worker dose limits, you will learn about methods of managing and monitoring internal exposure during the early phase. There are two methods to do so:

- Monitoring with Time and Turn-Back Limits
- Administering Potassium Iodide

During the next section of this lesson you will learn about each of these methods.

Monitoring Internal Exposure: Time and Turn-Back Limits (1 of 2)

The PAG subcommittee provides three options for monitoring internal exposure using dose limits. Select the links below to learn more about these options.

1. Use minimal control of inhalation dose from particulate materials during evacuation; that is, calculate CEDE after the fact once a spectrum of the radionuclides is available.

o   Definition: Option 1 is to control only the whole-body gamma and thyroid dose during evacuation.
o   Rationale: It is not practical to rotate workers. Also, the inhalation dose is controlled for tasks after evacuation and evacuation may be completed before plume arrives (ideal situation).
o   Disadvantages: The risk of overexposure is higher than for other options.
2.   Use previously established administrative dose limits; that is, use an emergency worker factor of five or some other dose correction factor (DCF).
o   Definition: Option 2 involves using pre-established administrative limits. This is also called the "mission limit."
o   Rationale: It is easy to implement. Once the limit is reached, pull out workers or authorize additional dose. Also it will meet limits for most probable accidents.
o   Disadvantages: It may not provide adequate control for the most severe accidents.
3.   Use contextually calculated dose limits based on analysis of isotopes in the plume. Select this link to access a summary of the information presented on this screen.
o   Definition: Option 3 recommends calculating contextual mission limits applicable to the accident in progress. This requires analysis of the isotopes and their concentrations in the plume.
o   Rationale: This option is the most accurate means of measuring dose correction factor. The same can be said of data for dose projection. Mission limits would be more defensible.
o   Disadvantages: Necessary data may not/will not be available particularly early in an event.

Monitoring Internal Exposure: Time and Turn-Back Limits (2 of 2)

The table accessible below lists the dosimeter adjustment factors for different accident categories. It shows the difference between the TEDE dose and an EDE dose based on the external dosimeter reading.

The individual's TEDE dose could be up to 37 times higher than what the dosimeter indicates. If a pocket chamber dosimeter reads 1 R, the TEDE would be approximately 37 rem.

Managing Internal Exposure: Administering Potassium Iodide (KI)

You will learn more about the use of KI in Lesson 8. State and county health officers determine KI availability and proper use for their jurisdictions.

Lesson Summary

Let's summarize what you have learned in this lesson:

- Examples of categories that may be designated as emergency workers include law enforcement, firefighting, radiation protection, civil defense, emergency management traffic control, health services, transportation services, and animal care.
- Emergency worker dose limits and protective action guides (PAGs) are not the same. PAGs are not limits; they are projected doses that warrant taking a protective action
- Emergency worker dose limits are based on a federally acceptable level of risk of health effects and may be adjusted based on the collective dose to the population being protected.

- Intermediate-phase dose limits are the same as occupational worker does limits.
- During the early phase, internal exposure can be managed by administration of KI and monitored using direct-reading dosimeters.

The next lesson will cover considerations that must go into the use of potassium iodide (KI) as a supplemental public protective action.

Lesson 8: KI as a Supplemental Public Protective Action

Lesson Overview

The purpose of this lesson is to provide an overview of the use of potassium iodide (KI) as a supplemental public protective action.

Upon completion of this lesson, you will be able to:

- Describe Federal policy regarding the use of KI as a thyroidal blocking agent by emergency workers, institutionalized persons, and the general public.
- Describe FDA recommendation for administration of KI based on age, predicted thyroid exposure, and pregnancy and lactation status.
- Explain Federal guidelines associated with the decision making process concerning KI as a supplemental public protective action.

Remember you can access the glossary in one of two ways throughout this course. You can select the glossary button in the top right hand corner of each main content screen. In addition, on content screens you can select underlined words to access their definitions in the online glossary. Selecting an underlined word will take you directly to its definition in the glossary.

This lesson should take approximately **45 minutes** to complete.

Implementation of KI References

NRC amended 10 CFR 50.47 (10)

NRC amended 10 CFR 50.47 (10) (1 of 2)

On January 19, 2001, the Nuclear Regulatory Commission (NRC) published an amendment to its regulations, 10 CFR 50.47 (10), requiring that consideration be given to including KI as a protective measure for the general public that would supplement sheltering and evacuation.

NRC amended 10 CFR 50.47 (10) (2 of 2)

Any licensee (plant operator) has an obligation to ensure that states have considered the use of KI as a supplemental protective action for the public. Licensees are required to use this information in developing protective action recommendations for off-site agencies.

If states make the decision to make KI available for the public, the NRC will fund supplies for two tablets per individual within the 10-mile EPZ. The NRC will not fund ancillary costs, including storage or distribution.

Implementation References

Current references on implementation include: FRPCC Federal Policy.

Federal Radiological Preparedness Coordinating Committee (FRPCC) Policy

The FRPCC has revised the 1985 Federal policy regarding the use of KI as a thyroidal blocking agent by emergency workers, institutionalized persons, and the general public in the vicinity of nuclear power plants. This policy is for use by state, Native American tribal nations, and local agencies responsible for radiological emergency planning and preparedness in the unlikely event of a major radiological emergency at a commercial nuclear power plant.

Federal position on Use of KI - The Federal position is that KI should be stockpiled and distributed to emergency workers and institutionalized persons for radiological emergencies at a nuclear power plant and its use should be considered for the general public within the 10-mile EPZ of a nuclear power plant. However, the decision on whether to use KI for the general public is left to the discretion of states and, in some cases, local governments.

In making the decision whether to stockpile KI, the states should be aware that the Federal government believes that the use of KI is reasonable and prudent measure as a supplemental protective action for the public. While there may be logistical difficulties in providing KI to the general public, any distribution scheme should take care to ensure that KI distribution does not impede or delay orderly evacuation.

Chernobyl accident's Impact on FRPCC policy - Revision of the policy to include members of the public reflects lessons learned from the Chernobyl Nuclear power plant accident of 1986, both about the consequences of an accident and about the safety and efficacy of KI.

The Chernobyl accident demonstrated that thyroid cancer can indeed be a major result of a large reactor accident. Based on the experiences from Chernobyl, young children are at greatest risk of thyroid cancer from radioactive iodine exposure. The critical exposure pathway was consumption of contaminated milk as previous lessons have stated.

There may be a few medical side effects in administering the drug to potentially affected individuals or in administering the drug to the general public in a radiological emergency. Although the post-Chernobyl data from Poland revealed few serious medical side effects associated with this drug, this possibility cannot be discounted, especially in certain groups of people. For example, people who are allergic to iodine should not take KI.

Implementation References

Current references on implementation include: FEMA, *Guidance on the Use of KI by the General Public for Commercial Nuclear Power Plant Accidents.*

FEMA Guidelines for KI Implementation

The decision to include KI in the range of public protective actions rests with the states. FEMA is available to assist states with the decision making process and has developed a decision matrix to aid in that process. There are two basic methods of distribution:

- Pre-distribution to the public
- Stockpiles in facilities such as reception or mass care centers

Based on the distribution method adopted by a state, the capability to implement the decision will be evaluated by FEMA as part of its "Reasonable Assurance Finding" recommendation to the NRC. The evaluation of a states' capability to distribute KI to the general public can be achieved through the Annual Letter of Certification, when KI is pre-distributed, and/or a combination of Staff Assistance Visits and biennial exercise demonstrations, when KI is in a fixed facility.

Implementation References

Current references on implementation include: *Guidance on the Use of KI as a Thyroid Blocking Agent in Radiation Emergencies.*

FDA, Guidance on the Use of KI as a Thyroid Blocking Agent in Radiation Emergencies

FDA guidance on the use of KI as a thyroid blocking agent in radiation emergencies has been updated from its original content in 1978.

The latest guidance was revised based upon a comprehensive review of the data relating radioiodine exposure to thyroid cancer risk accumulated in the aftermath of the 1986 Chernobyl reactor accident.

The studies support the etiologic role of relatively small doses of radioiodine in the dramatic increase in thyroid cancer among exposed children. Furthermore, it appears that the increased risk occurs with a relatively short latency. Finally, the Polish experience supports the use of KI as a safe and effective means by which to protect against thyroid cancer caused by internal thyroid irradiation from inhalation of contaminated air or ingestion of contaminated food and drink when exposure cannot be prevented by evacuation, sheltering, or food, and milk control.

Latest Guidance: Risks of Stable Iodine Administration

Short-term administration of KI at thyroid blocking doses is safe and, in general, more so in children than adults. The risks of stable iodine administration include sialadenitis (an inflammation of the salivary gland), gastrointestinal disturbances, allergic reactions, and minor rashes. In addition, persons with known iodine sensitivity should avoid KI, as should individuals with dermatitus herpetiformis and hypocomplementemic vasculitis, extremely rare conditions associated with an increased risk of iodine hypersensitivity.

Thyroidal side effects of stable iodine include iodine-induced thyrotoxicosis, which is more common in older people and in iodine deficient areas but usually requires repeated doses of stable iodine. In addition, iodide goiter and hypothyroidism are potential side effects more common in iodine sufficient areas, but they require chronic higher doses of stable iodine. In light of the preceding, individuals with multinodular goiter, Graves' disease, and autoimmune thyroiditis should be treated with caution, especially if dosing extends beyond a few days. The vast majority of such individuals will be adults. The transient hypothyroidism observed in 0.37% (12 of 3214) of neonates (newborn child) treated with KI in Poland after Chernobyl has been without reported sequelae to date (pathological conditions following the initial effect). There is no question that the benefits of KI treatment to reduce the risk of thyroid cancer outweigh the risks of such treatment in neonates. Nevertheless, in light of the potential consequences of even transient hypothyroidism for intellectual development, the FDA recommends that neonates (within the first month of life) treated with KI be monitored for this effect by measurement of TSH (and FT4, if indicated) and that thyroid hormone therapy be instituted in cases in which hypothyroidism develops.

Latest Guidance: FDA Recommendation for Administration of KI

Recommendations of KI administration for different risk groups are meant to provide states and local authorities as well as other agencies with the best current guidance on safe and effective use of KI to reduce thyroidal radioiodine exposure and thus the risk of thyroid cancer. The FDA recognizes that, in the event of an emergency, some or all of the specific dosing recommendations may be very difficult to carry out given their complexity and the logistics of implementation of a program of KI distribution. The recommendations should therefore be interpreted with flexibility as necessary to allow optimally effective and safe dosing given the exigencies of any particular emergency situation.

- **Adults over 40 years** - Adults over 40 need take KI only in the case of a projected large internal radiation dose to the thyroid (> 500 rem) to prevent hypothyroidism. The downward KI dose adjustment by age group, based on body size considerations, adheres to the principle of minimum effective dose.
- **Adults over 18 through 40 years** - The recommended standard dose of KI for adults through age 40 is same as adults over 40 and adolescents (130 mg).
- **Adolescents over 12 through 18 years** - Adolescents approaching adult size (i.e.,>70 kg) should receive the full adult dose (130 mg).
- **Children over 3 through 12 years** - The recommended standard dose of KI for all school-age children is the same (65 mg).
- **Children over 1 month through 3 years** - The standard dose of KI for children over 1 month through 3 years is 32 mg.
- **Birth through 1 month** - Neonates should receive the lowest dose (16 mg). Repeat dosing of neonates should be avoided.
- **Pregnant or lactating women** - Pregnant women should be given KI for their own protection and for that of the fetus, as iodine readily crosses the placenta. However, because of the risk of

blocking fetal thyroid function with excess iodine, repeat dosing with KI of pregnant women should be avoided.

Lactating females should be administered KI for their own protection, as for other young adults, and potentially to reduce the radioiodine content of the breast milk, but not as a means to deliver KI to infants, who should get their KI directly. As for direct administration of KI, stable iodine as a component of breast milk may also pose a risk of hypothyroidism in nursing neonates. Therefore, repeat dosing with KI should be avoided in the lactating mother, except during continuing severe contamination.

Latest Guidance: Dosage of KI Administration

The protective effect of KI lasts approximately 24 hours. For optimal prophylaxis, KI should therefore be dosed daily, until a risk of significant exposure to radioiodines by either inhalation or ingestion no longer exists.

The following people should be given priority with regard to other protective measures (i.e., sheltering, evacuation, and control of the food supply):

- Individuals intolerant of KI at protective doses
- Neonates
- Pregnant women
- Lactating women

Latest Guidance: Timing of KI Administration

For optimal protection against inhaled radioiodines, KI should be administered before or immediately coincident with passage of the radioactive cloud, though KI may still have a substantial protective effect even if taken 3 or 4 hours after exposure. Furthermore, if the release of radioiodines into the atmosphere is protracted, then, of course, even delayed administration may reap benefits by reducing, if incompletely, the total radiation dose to the thyroid.

Prevention of thyroid uptake of ingested radioiodines, once the plume has passed and radiation protection measures (including KI) are in place, is best accomplished by food control measures and not by repeated administration of KI. Because of radioactive decay, grain products, and canned milk or vegetables from sources affected by radioactive fallout, if stored for weeks to months after production, pose no radiation risk from radioiodine. Thus, late KI prophylaxis at the time of consumption is not required.

Implementation References

Current references on implementation include: *Home Preparation Procedure for Emergency Administration of KI Tablets to Infants and Small Children.*

FDA, Home Preparation Procedure for Emergency Administration of KI Tablets to Infants and Small Children (1 of 2)

KI is stockpiled as tablets because tablets are easy to store; however, infants and small children cannot swallow tablets. In an emergency, KI may need to be given to infants and small children by their parents or caregivers. Since KI dissolved in water may be too salty to drink, the FDA is providing instructions on how to mix the KI tablets with food or drink to disguise the taste.

Taste tests were conducted with six mixtures of KI and drinks:
- Water
- Low fat milk
- Low fat chocolate milk
- Flat soda (e.g. cola)
- Raspberry syrup
- Orange juice

The mixture of KI and **raspberry syrup** disguised the taste best. Low fat chocolate milk, orange juice, and flat soda generally had an acceptable taste. Low fat white milk and water did not hide the salty taste.

FDA, Home Preparation Procedure for Emergency Administration of KI Tablets to Infants and Small Children (2 of 2)

To administer KI tablets to infants and small children at home, you will need the appropriate ingredients and supplies.

Ingredients and supplies needed:
- 130 mg KI tablet
- Metal spoon
- Small bowl
- One of the drinks from the list or infant formula

Mixture preparation:
- Grind one 130 mg tablet into a fine powder in bowl with metal spoon.
- Add four teaspoonfuls of water. Mix with spoon until dissolved.
- Add four teaspoonfuls of drink to the mixture.

The amount of KI in the drink is 16.25 mg per teaspoon. The number of teaspoons administered depends on the age of the child. The mixture will keep for up to seven days in the refrigerator. The FDA recommends that KI drink mixtures be prepared weekly; unused portions should be discarded.

Implementation References

Current references on implementation include: FDA, *DRAFT Guidance for Federal Agencies and State and Local Governments*, KI Tablets Shelf Life Extension.

FDA, DRAFT Guidance: KI Tablets Shelf Life Extension (1 of 3)

This document is intended to provide guidance to Federal agencies and to state and local governments on testing to extend the shelf life of stockpiled KI tablets. The FDA developed this document in response to several state inquiries on this topic.

This guidance discusses the FDA recommendations on:

- The requisite testing for such shelf life extensions
- The qualifications of laboratories suitable to conduct the tests
- The issues regarding notification of holders of stockpiled KI tablets as well as end users (consumers who have purchased KI, or intermediate holders of KI such as fire departments, health departments, hospitals, or other entities who store KI for use in emergencies) about changes to batch shelf life once testing has been successfully conducted.

This guidance is applicable for KI that is stockpiled under controlled conditions.

FDA, DRAFT Guidance: KI Tablets Shelf Life Extension (2 of 3)

KI tablets, USP, is a compendial drug product that is manufactured to meet the recommended tests and specifications listed in the USP monograph. Assay and dissolution are the two specifications with potential relevance to stability, assuming identification and content uniformity testing were performed at release.

Identification and content uniformity are performed by the quality control division of the manufacturer before the product can be released for sale. Stability studies over many years have confirmed that none of the components of KI tablets, including the active ingredient, has any significant potential for chemical degradation or interaction with other components or with the components of the container closure system when stored per labeled directions.

FDA, DRAFT Guidance: KI Tablets Shelf Life Extension (3 of 3)

To date, the only observed changes during stability testing have been the failure of some batches of KI tablets to meet the USP S1 dissolution specification, Q=75 percent in 15 minutes. Some tablets tested required slightly longer than the specified time to achieve dissolution. Even in the case of a failure of this sort, the product would remain stable. In such cases, instructions can be provided to crush the tablets and mix them with juice or other liquid prior to administration as suggested for emergency pediatric dosing.

In any long-term stability evaluation, appearance should be monitored as a matter of course. In the specific case of KI tablets, a yellowish discoloration would be indicative of stability problems. Since pure KI is known to be very stable (as long as it is protected from moist air), ongoing evaluation and testing of each batch is probably unnecessary as long as the market package remains intact and continues to be stored under controlled conditions as described in the labeling.

Implementation References

Current references on implementation include: FEMA, *REP Program Manual.*

FEMA, REP Program Manual, August 2002

According to FEMA policy, criterion 2.b.2. a decision-making process involving consideration of appropriate factors and necessary coordination is used to make protective action decisions (PADs) for the general public (including the recommendation for the use of KI, if it is the Off-site Response Organization's [ORO] policy).

If the ORO has determined that KI will be used as a protective measure for the general public under off-site plans, then the ORO should demonstrate the capability to make decisions on the distribution and administration of KI as a protective measure for the general public to supplement sheltering and evacuation. This decision should be based on the ORO's plan and procedures or projected thyroid dose compared with the established PAG for KI administration. The KI decisionmaking process should involve close coordination with appropriate assessment and decision-making staff.

Implementation References

Current references on implementation include:
- NRC Amended 10 CFR 50.47(10) 1/19/01
- FRPCC Federal Policy, 1/10/02
- FEMA. Guidance on the Use of KI by the General Public for Commercial Nuclear Power Plant Accidents, 12/20/01
- FDA Guidance on the Use of KI as a Thyroid Blocking Agent in Radiation Emergencies, 12/11/01
- FDA Home Preparation Procedure for Emergency Administration of KI Tablets to Infacnts and Small Children 7/3/02
- FDA DRAFT Guidance for Federal Agencies and State and Local Governments, KI Tablets Shelf Life Extension, 3/03
- FEMA, REP Program Manual, 4.12

You have reviewed all current references on implementation of KI as supplemental public protective action.

Lesson Summary

In this lesson you learned about the following references that provide guidance on using KI as a supplemental public protective action:
- NRC Amended 10 CFR 50.47 (10)
- FRPCC policy

- FEMA, Guidance on the Use of KI by the General Public for Commercial Nuclear Power Plant Accidents
- FDA, Guidance on the Use of KI as a Thyroid Blocking Agent in Radiation Emergencies
- FDA, Home Preparation Procedure for Emergency Administration of KI Tablets to Infants and Small Children
- FDA, Draft Guidance for Federal Agencies and State and Local Governments, KI Tablets Shelf Life Extension
- FEMA, REP Program Manual

The next lesson will cover FDA protective action guides (PAGs).

Lesson 9: FDA PAGs and Ingestion Pathway Protective Actions

Lesson Overview

The purpose of this lesson is to provide an overview of FDA Protective Action Guides (PAGs).

- Upon completion of this lesson, you will be able to:
- Describe the role, responsibilities, and response capabilities of the United States Department of Agriculture (USDA) in the intermediate phase of a nuclear power plant accident.
- Define the ingestion pathway zone.
- Describe the measures recommended by USDA to be taken by food producers, processors, and transporters to prevent the contamination of foodstuffs and to protect the public from ingestion of contaminated agricultural products.
- Define derived intervention level (DIL) and describe the process of applying DILs.

Remember you can access the glossary in one of two ways throughout this course. You can select the glossary button in the top right hand corner of each main content screen. In addition, on content screens you can select underlined words to access their definitions in the online glossary. Selecting an underlined word will take you directly to its definition in the glossary.

This lesson should take approximately **1 hour** to complete.

FDA Protective Action Guides (PAGs)

On August 13, 1998, the U.S Food and Drug Administration (FDA) issued a guidance document entitled Accidental Radioactive Contamination of Human Food and Animal Feeds: Recommendations for State and Local Agencies. The FDA has a responsibility for issuing guidance on planning actions for evaluating and preventing contamination of human food or animal feeds and on the control and use of these products should they become contaminated.

To facilitate implementation of the FDA PAGs during an incident, the National Response Framework (NRF) has assigned the United States Department of Agriculture (USDA) the responsibility for providing assistance to state and local governments in developing agricultural protective action recommendations and in providing agricultural damage assessments. You will learn more about USDA's role later in this lesson.

The FEMA REP Program Manual, April 2012 also provides guidance on implementation of the FDA PAGs.

FDA PAG Values

The FDA PAGs are:

- 5 mSv (0.5 rem) for committed effective dose equivalent (CEDE); or
- 50 mSv (5 rem) for committed dose equivalent (CDE) to an individual tissue or organ, whichever is the more limiting

The current nominal estimate for the general population for lifetime total cancer mortality for low-LET (linear energy transfer) ionizing radiation, delivered at low doses and low dose rates, is approximately 1 in 200 for a reference dose equivalent in the whole body of 100 mSv (10 rem). For 5 mSv (0.5 rem) CEDE, the associated lifetime cancer mortality would be 2.25 x 10-4 or approximately 1 in 5000.

For comparison, the estimate of the normal total cancer mortality rate in the United States for the general population, not associated with additional radiation doses from ingestion of contaminated food from an accident, is 1.9x10-1 or approximately 1 in 5. For example, in a general population of 10,000 individuals, each receiving a dose of 5 mSv (0.5 rem) CEDE, the number of cancer deaths in that population of individuals could increase, in theory, by about 2 cancer deaths over the lifetimes of the individuals—that is, from the expected number of 1900 to 1902.

FDA PAG Recommendations

For a nuclear power plant incident, the foundation planning requirement document, the updated NUREG-0654 states the following in criteria J.9. "Each State and local government shall establish a capability to implement protective measures based on protective action guides and other criteria."

It further states in part, "This shall be consistent with the recommendations of...with those of DHEW (HHS)/FDA regarding radioactive contamination of human food and animal feeds..." Alternative approaches may be used if such approaches satisfy the applicable statute, regulations, or both.

The recommendations advise that health risk to the public should be averted by limiting the radiation dose received as a result of consumption of accidentally contaminated food. This should be accomplished by:

- Setting derived intervention levels (DILs) on the radionuclide activity concentration permitted in human food.
- Taking protective actions to reduce the amount of contamination.

You will learn about derived intervention levels (DILs) later in this lesson. Next, you will learn more about protective actions.

Preventive Protective Actions (1 of 2)

Preventive protective actions are actions taken to prevent or reduce contamination of water, milk and food products. Protective actions should be initiated subject to evaluation of the situation and should continue until, in the absence of the actions, the concentrations remain below the DILs. Protective actions can be taken to:

- Avoid or limit, through precautionary measures, the amount of contamination that could become incorporated in human food and animal feeds.
- Delay or limit consumption of human food and animal feeds suspected of being contaminated until the concentration of contamination has been determined.
- Reduce the amount of contamination in human food and animal feeds.

Precautionary actions should be implemented to avoid placing in jeopardy persons implementing the actions. For example, in the case of an accident involving a commercial nuclear power plant, if the predictions of the magnitude of future off-site contamination are persuasive, precautionary actions might need to be taken and completed prior to declaration of a general emergency (GE).

The FDA guidance does not provide limits on concentrations that should be permitted in animal feeds. However, protective actions for animal feeds are included as measures to reduce or prevent subsequent contamination of human food.

Preventive Protective Actions (2 of 2)

Sample analysis will be required to quantify contamination.

- **Milk**
  - Remove lactating animals from pasture and place in shelter. Use feed from enclosed silos, granaries, or barns
  - Withhold contaminated milk from market
  - Store for prolonged periods of time to allow for radioactive decay. Fluid milk may be kept for long periods of time using ultra-high-temperature pasteurization
  - Divert fluid milk. Milk may be used for manufactured milk products such as cheese, butter, and dried milk
- **Fruits and Vegetables**
  - Cover exposed products, when possible
  - Remove surface contamination by washing and peeling
  - Preserve fruits and vegetables by canning, freezing or dehydration
- **Meat and Meat Products**
  - Place animals on uncontaminated feed and water and place in shelter
- **Poultry and Poultry Products**
  - Poultry being raised indoors are probably not contaminated
  - Free-range poultry should be placed on uncontaminated feed and water and placed in shelter
- **Soils**
  - Idle or dispose
  - Alternate crops (substitute other crops that contribute little or no contamination to the human diet, such as cotton)
  - Plow deeply (radioactive contamination is moved well below the root levels of crops to prevent uptake)
  - Lime (limits root uptake)
- **Grains**

- o   Mill and polish to remove hulls
  - o   Allow to weather (remain in the field where some natural decay will occur)
  - o   Store separately from previously harvested grain
- **Water**
  - o   Cover open wells, rain barrels and tanks
  - o   Disconnect filler pipes from runoff supplies
  - o   Close water intake valves from contaminated sources
- **Fish and Marine Life**
  - o   Close the fishing season. This includes lakes, rivers, and ponds (public and private)
  - o   Prevent harvesting of seafood
- **Honey**
  - o   Stop collection of honey
  - o   Stop cross-pollination
- **Game and Wildlife**
  - o   Close hunting season
- **Additional Considerations**
  - o   Notify food processors, distributors and farmers
  - o   Initiate quarantine and/or embargo procedures
    - ▪   Develop food control area to isolate contaminated products
    - ▪   Develop food control points to prevent transfer of contaminated products from one area to another
  - o   Develop sampling strategy plan for intermediate and long term
    - ▪   Sampling must be done often and repetitively
    - ▪   Provide appropriate laboratory support
    - ▪   Decide if farmers can reenter contaminated area as radiation workers
    - ▪   Obtain Federal assistance
    - ▪   Consider insurance and indemnification issues
    - ▪   Develop recovery plan, including reentry, relocation and return

USDA Response Role

As you learned earlier in this lesson, USDA is responsible for facilitating implementation of the FDA PAGs during an incident. In the next section of this lesson, you will learn more about USDA's specific role.

The USDA's major concern is food safety. In response to a radiological emergency, the USDA's Food Safety and Inspection Service assumes the lead USDA agency role.

The principal USDA role is to provide guidance and assistance to state and local governments. USDA advisors will assist state and local officials, in coordination with the Department of Health and Human Services (HHS) and the EPA, in recommending and implementing of agricultural protective actions to limit or prevent the ingestion of contaminated food.

The USDA will provide assistance to assess damage to crops, soil, livestock, poultry, and processing facilities from radiological contamination. It will incorporate findings into a damage assessment report.

USDA National Response Framework (NRF) Responsibilities

Under the National Response Framework (NRF), the USDA is responsible for:

- Inspection of meat and meat products, poultry and poultry products, and egg products identified for interstate and foreign commerce to ensure that they are safe for human consumption.
- Assistance in monitoring the production, processing, storage, and distribution of food through the wholesale level to eliminate contaminated products or to reduce the contamination in the products to a safe level.
- Collection of agricultural samples within the ingestion pathway zone.
- Assistance in the evaluation and assessment of data to determine the impact of the emergency on agriculture.

Advisory Team for Environment, Food, and Health

USDA personnel, along with EPA, HHS, and other Federal agencies as needed, will serve on the Advisory Team for Environment, Food, and Health. The Advisory Team will convene for SAE incidents and above. This team will provide a mechanism for timely interagency coordination of advice and recommendations to the state agency and lead federal agency (LFA) concerning:

- Environmental assessments (field monitoring)
- PAGs and their application to the emergency
- Data and assessment from the Federal Radiological Monitoring and Assessment Center (FRMAC)
- Preventing or minimizing the contamination of milk, food, and water and exposure through ingestion
- Disposition of contaminated livestock and poultry
- Minimizing losses of agricultural resources from radiation effects
- Availability of food, animal feed and water supply inspection programs to ensure wholesomeness
- Relocation, reentry and other radiation protection measures prior to recovery
- Recovery, return, and cleanup issues
- Health and safety advice or information for the public and for workers
- Estimates of effects of radioactive releases on human health and environment
- The use of radioprotective substances (e.g., thyroid blocking agents), including dosage and projected radiation doses that warrant the use of such drugs
- Other matters, as requested by the Coordinating Agency

The Federal Radiological Monitoring and Assessment Center (FRMAC)

The Advisory Team is usually collocated with the Federal Radiological Monitoring and Assessment Center, or FRMAC. For emergencies with potential for causing widespread radiological contamination where no on-scene FRMAC is established, the functions of the Advisory Team may be accomplished in the coordinating agency response facility in Washington, DC.

The Advisory Team will not release information or make recommendations to the public unless authorized to do so by the coordinating agency.

Other USDA personnel will also assist DOE/EPA at the FRMAC with:

- Information on current harvesting to set sampling priorities.
- Collection of agricultural samples.

Ingestion Pathway Zone

Now that you have learned about the FDA PAGs, you will learn about how contamination occurs through the ingestion exposure pathways.

The ingestion pathway zone is the area approximately within a 50 mile radius of a nuclear power plant. In the ingestion pathway zone, radionuclides may be deposited on crops, vegetation, bodies of surface water, and ground surfaces. The resulting contaminated food and water may present a risk to the public and to livestock.

Potential Ingestion Pathways

There are three ingestion pathways.

- Food - Four potential pathways have been identified by which radionuclides released during an accident may contaminate food supplies:
    - Direct deposition on edible plants
    - Deposition via contaminated irrigation water
    - Uptake by plants from soil
    - Deposition on edible plants by resuspension of radionuclides deposited on soil
- Water - The pathways resulting in contamination of potable water supplies are:
    - Airborne plume deposition on surface water
    - Runoff from soil or snow contaminated by plume
    - Leaching and/or migration of radioactive fluids to water supplies
    - Direct release of contaminated effluents to a river or other water body that supplies drinking or irrigation water
- Milk - One pathway has been identified that results in contamination of the milk supply: airborne plume deposition on pasture, ingestion of contaminated feed by cow, and concentration of radionuclides in milk. Although radionuclides such as Cs-134, Cs-137, Sr-89 and Sr-90 may result in doses through the milk pathway, the I-131 dose will probably be larger than that of each of the other nuclides.

Derived Intervention Levels (DILs) (1 of 2)

Earlier in this lesson, you learned that protective actions should be initiated and continue until concentrations of contamination are below the Derived Intervention Levels (DILs). You will now learn about why they are established and how they are calculated.

DILs are limits on the concentrations of radionuclides permitted in human food distributed in commerce. DILs are also recommended for non-commercial products. They are established to prevent consumption of undesirable amounts of radionuclides and are expressed in units of radionuclide activity per kilogram of food, i.e., Becquerel per kilogram (Bq/kg).

Although the basic PAG recommendations are given in terms of projected dose equivalent, it is often more convenient to use specific radionuclide concentrations as the basis for protective actions.

Derived Intervention Levels (DILs) (2 of 2)

A DIL is the concentration of a radionuclide in food that would lead to an individual's receiving a dose equal to the PAG. DILs establish limits on the radionuclide activity permitted in human food.

DILs are calculated in becquerels per kilogram and are derived by dividing the intervention level of dose by the product of the fraction of food assumed to be contaminated, the quantity of food consumed, and the dose received per unit of activity.

The FDA DILs provide a large margin of safety for the public because each DIL is set according to a conservative scenario for the most vulnerable group of individuals. In addition, protective actions would be taken if radionuclide concentrations were to reach or exceed a DIL at any point in time, even though such concentrations would need to be sustained throughout the relevant extended period of time for the radiation dose to actually reach the PAG.

DIL = PAG / [(f) (food intake) (DC)]

- DIL = Derived Intervention Level, Bq/kg
- PAG = Protective Action Guide, mSv
- f = Fraction of food assumed contaminated
- Food Intake = Quantity of food consumed, kg
- DC = Dose received per unit of activity, mSv/Bq

DIL Applicability (1 of 2)

Accident types for which DILs were developed:

- **Nuclear Reactors** - The results of food monitoring by the FDA and others following the Chernobyl accident support the conclusion that I-131, Cs-134, and Cs-137 are the principal radionuclides that contribute to radiation dose by ingestion following a nuclear reactor accident, but that Ru-103 and Ru-106 also should be included in considerations. The use of DILs was shown to be a practical way to control the radiation dose from ingestion of food that has been contaminated as a result of a nuclear reactor accident.

- **Nuclear Fuel Reprocessing Plants -** Nuclides of concern from a fuel reprocessing plant accident resulting in contamination of the environment include: Sr-90, Cs-137, Pu-239, and Am-241. Plutonium and Americium are alpha emitters.
- **Nuclear Waste Storage Facilities -** Sr-90, Cs-137, Pu-239, and Am-241 are also of concern at nuclear waste storage facilities.
- **Nuclear Weapons -** Without nuclear detonation, Pu-239 is the only nuclide released during this type of accident. Pu-239 half-life is 2.411×10^4 years.
- **Radioisotope Thermoelectric Generators and Radioisotope Heater Units Used in Space Vehicles -** Pu-238 decay provides power for many spacecraft.
- **All Other Contamination -** In unique circumstances, such as transportation accidents, other radionuclides may contribute radiation doses through the food ingestion pathway. These situations are not specifically addressed in the FDA recommendations. An evaluation of the radiation dose from ingestion of these other radionuclides should be performed, however, to determine if the PAGs would be exceeded. The FDA guidance provides guidance for these "minor isotopes".

DILs apply during the first year after an accident. If there is concern that food will continue to be significantly contaminated beyond the first year, the long-term circumstances need to be evaluated to determine whether the DILs should be continued or if other guidance may be more applicable.

DIL Applicability (2 of 2)

Food with concentrations below the DILs is permitted to move in commerce without restrictions. Food with concentrations at or above the DILs is not normally permitted into commerce. However, state and local officials have flexibility in deciding whether or not to apply restrictions in special circumstances, such as permitting use of food by a population group with a unique dependency on certain food types.

Recommended DILs (1 of 2)

Each DIL applies to the sum of the concentrations of the radionuclides in the group at the time of measurement, rounded up to two significant figures.

Note: Divide Ru-103 by 6800 and divide Ru-106 by 450. If the sum is less than or equal to 1, the food is edible; if the sum is greater than 1, the food is inedible.

The PAG of 5 mSv (0.5 rem) CEDE is most limiting for Cs-134 + Cs-137 and Ru-103 + Ru-106. The PAG of 50 mSv (5 rem) CDE to a single specific tissue or organ is most limiting for Sr-90, I-131, and Pu-238 + Pu-239 + Am-241.

Recommended DILs (2 of 2)

The recommended DILs for each radionuclide group are applicable to foods as prepared for consumption. For dried or concentrated products such as powdered milk or concentrated juices, adjust by a factor appropriate to reconstitution, and assume the reconstitution water is not contaminated. For spices, which are consumed in very small quantities, use a dilution factor of 10.

Now that you have learned about the recommended DILs, you will learn about the assumptions upon which these recommendations were based.

DIL Assumptions: Age Groups

The DILs were calculated for six age groups using protective action guides, dose coefficients, and dietary intakes, including tap water for drinking, relevant to each radionuclide and age group. The age groups included:

- 3 months
- 1 year
- 5 years
- 10 years
- 15 years and adult (>17 years)

Protection of the more vulnerable segments of the population and the practicality of implementation were major considerations in the selection of DILs. These considerations led to the selection of a single DIL for each radionuclide group based on the most limiting PAG and age group for the radionuclide group.

There are different DILs for infant and adult because the different body weights and organ sizes as well as the percentage of total dietary intake of a particular food will influence the severity of the dose received.

DIL Assumptions: Fractions Assumed to be Contaminated

The DIL calculations presume that contamination will occur in 30% of the dietary intake. The value of 30% was chosen based on the expectation that normally less than 10% of the annual dietary intake of most members of the population would consist of contaminated food.

An additional factor of three was applied to account for limited subpopulations that might be more dependent on local food supplies.

An exception was made for I-131 in the diets of the three-month and one-year age groups, where the entire intake over a 60-day period was assumed to be contaminated (because the diet for these age groups consists of a high percentage of milk).

Therefore, $f = 0.3$, except for I-131 in infants, where $f = 1.0$.

DIL Assumptions: Food Intake

Food intake includes all dietary components for each age group, including tap water used for drinking, and is the overall quantity consumed in one year.

There are exceptions in the period of time for I-131 and Ru-103 due to the more rapid decay of these radionuclides.

- I-131: 60 days since its half-life is 8.04 days
- Ru-103: 280 days since its half-life is 39.3 days

Dietary intakes were derived from EPA and USDA data.

DIL Assumptions: Dose Coefficients

The dose coefficients used, in mSv/Bq, were taken from ICRP Publication 56 (ICRP 1989). The most limiting dose from each of the nine radionuclides per age group was used in the calculation to arrive at the DIL. Ru-103 and Ru-106 are chemically identical; however, their widely differing half-lives (39.3 days and 373 days, respectively) result in markedly differing individual DILs that do not permit simple averaging.

Example: Calculating the DIL for Cs-134 and Cs-137:

$$DIL\ (Bq/kg) = \frac{PAG(mSv)}{(f) \times (food\ intake\ in\ kg) \times (dose\ coefficient\ in\ \frac{mSv}{Bq})}$$

where:

- $f = 0.3$ for all except I-131

- Food intake = 943 kg (largest annual intake of all age groups was adult),

- Dose coefficient = 1.9×10^{-5} for Cs-134, 1.3×10^{-5} for Cs-137 (for adults since they had the largest dietary intake)

- PAG = 5 mSv CEDE (most limiting PAG for Cs group)

$$DIL\ (Bq/kg) = \frac{5\ mSv}{(0.3) \times (943\ kg) \times (1.9 \times 10^{-5}\ \frac{mSv}{Bq})} = 930\ Bq/kg\ (Cs - 134)$$

$$= \frac{5\ mSv}{(0.3) \times (943\ kg) \times (1.3 \times 10^{-5}\ \frac{mSv}{Bq})} = 1360\ Bq/kg\ (Cs - 137)$$

$$930 + 1360 = 2290 / 2 = 1145 \approx 1200\ Bq/kg\ DIL\ (Cs\ group)$$

The answer should be rounded up to two significant figures, according to the PAG.

Implementation of Protective Actions

Now that you've learned about how DILs are established and how they guide protective actions, you will learn about protective actions that should be implemented before and after laboratory results arrive that confirm food contamination.

- **Prior to receiving laboratory results** - Protective actions that can be taken within an area likely to be affected before confirmation of contamination via laboratory results include:
    - Simple precautionary actions to avoid or reduce the potential for contamination of food and animal feeds prior to arrival of the contamination
    - Temporary embargoes to prevent the introduction into commerce of food that is likely to be contaminated. This action is appropriate only if there is significant expectation that contamination has occurred.

Protective actions can be taken before the release or arrival of contamination if there is advance knowledge that radionuclides may accidentally contaminate the environment. Simple precautionary actions include modest adjustment of normal operations before arrival of contamination. These will not guarantee that contamination in food will be below the DILs, but they will significantly reduce the severity of the problem.

Distribution and use of possibly contaminated food and animal feed is halted until the situation can be evaluated and monitoring and control actions instituted. Temporary embargoes are employed when the concentrations are not yet known. Because there is potential for negative impact on the community, justification for this action must be significant. Any embargo imposed should remain in effect at least until laboratory results are obtained. The geographical area under the embargo would depend on the accident sequence, the meteorological conditions, and the food affected.

- **After receiving laboratory results** - Protective actions that should be implemented when the contamination in the food equals or exceeds the DILs are:
    - Temporary embargoes to prevent the contaminated food from being introduced into commerce
    - Normal food production and processing actions that reduce the amount of contamination in or on food to levels below the DILs

Embargoes should continue until measured concentrations are below the DILs.

Normal food production and processing procedures that could reduce the amount of contamination in or on the food could be simple (e.g., holding to allow for decay, or removal of surface contamination by brushing, washing, or peeling) or could be complex. Blending of contaminated food with uncontaminated food is not permitted by law (adulteration).

Lesson Summary

Let's summarize what you have learned in this lesson:

- Before the arrival of the airborne plume, precautionary protective actions may be instituted to lessen the severity of contamination in milk, food, and water.
- The USDA is responsible for providing assistance to state and local governments in developing agricultural protective action recommendations and providing agricultural damage assessments.

- The ingestion pathway zone is the area approximately within a 50-mile radius of a nuclear power plant.
- Before confirmation of contamination, employment of temporary embargoes will limit the amount of contaminated food placed in commerce.
- DILs are concentrations of radionuclides in food that will cause a PAG to be exceeded.

The next lesson will provide an overview of field monitoring organization and protection.

Lesson 10: Field Monitoring Organization and Protection

Lesson Overview

In this lesson, you will learn about monitoring teams and their instruments as well as how to protect personnel in the field.

Upon completion of this lesson, you will be able to:

- Describe monitoring teams' organization, notification, communications, protection, and training requirements.
- List types of monitoring instruments and air sampling devices and what is measured by each.
- Identify measures to protect field sampling personnel and other critical workers from radiation.

Remember you can access the glossary in one of two ways throughout this course. You can select the glossary button in the top right hand corner of each main content screen. In addition, on content screens you can select underlined words to access their definitions in the online glossary. Selecting an underlined word will take you directly to its definition in the glossary.

This lesson should take approximately **45 minutes** to complete.

Introduction to Field Monitoring

In the event of an incident involving the release of radioactive material into the environment, radiological field monitoring is an important aspect of protecting the public. During a nuclear reactor accident, protective actions should be based initially upon plant conditions and then upon dose projections.

There are, however, many assumptions made in dose projections, and the estimated range of uncertainty between projected and actual off-site doses for severe accidents is at best within a factor of 10, and at worst, off by a factor of 100,000 [source: Nuclear Regulatory Commission Regulation NUREG-1210]. This makes field monitoring an essential requirement for public protection.

Requirements for Organization

Criteria for Preparation and Evacuation of Radiological Emergency Response Plans and Preparedness in Support of Nuclear Power Plants (NUREG-0654/FEMA REP-1), rev. 1 (October 1980) requires that each responsible organization "provide methods, equipment, and expertise to make rapid assessments of the actual or potential magnitude and locations of any radiological hazards through liquid or gaseous release pathways." This includes:

- Field Team Composition
- Means of Notification
- Estimated Deployment Times
- Communication
- Monitoring Capabilities
- Training Requirements

In this section of the lesson, you will learn what NUREG-0654 specifies for each of these key concepts.

Field Team Composition

According to NUREG-0654, each organization "shall be capable of continuous (24-hour) operations for a protracted period." Plans should specify:

- The number of teams required/available: A typical plan may use five to ten teams (a combination of licensee, state, and local).
- Makeup of those teams (minimum of two members per team): At least one person on the team should know the geography of the area. The availability of additional personnel to staff a second shift must be ensured for extended operations.
- Radiological training: All personnel assigned to monitoring teams will need training in monitoring plans, monitoring procedures, and sampling techniques.

State and local department of agriculture personnel are ideal candidates for the team because they are already trained in appropriate sampling techniques. Sampling procedures should be in place to reflect the laboratory needs for analyses.

State and local sampling teams may be augmented by Federal resources.

Requirements for Organization

Now that we have covered field team composition, you will learn about the means of notification requirements in NUREG-0654.

Means of Notification (1 of 2)

NUREG-0654 specifies:

- "Each organization shall provide for 24-hour per day emergency response, including 24-hour per day manning of communication links."
- "Each organization shall establish procedures for alerting, notifying, and mobilizing emergency response personnel."
- "Each organization shall establish reliable primary and backup means of communications . . . including provision for alerting or activating emergency personnel in each response organization."
- "Provide for updating telephone numbers in procedures at least quarterly."

Means of Notification (2 of 2)

To obtain the personnel necessary to perform field monitoring at any time of the day or night, on weekdays or weekends, the responsible organization must have the capability to alert and fully mobilize personnel.

Primary and backup notification systems should be available, operable and periodically tested. A "telephone tree" is often used to notify field team members when their services are needed. The listing for each member should include office, home and cellular telephone numbers. Pager numbers and the method of accessing the paging service should also be part of the listing as well as any ancillary notification methods. Including addresses in the listing, so that in-person contact can be initiated if communications systems fail, is a good idea, as is updating the list at least quarterly, as NUREG-0654 requires. Numbers, particularly area codes, change from time to time.

Requirements for Organization

Now you will learn about the estimated deployment time requirements in NUREG-0654.

Estimated Deployment Times

Technical staff members need to know the approximate response time of the field team so that they will know how soon they can expect data. Separate response time estimates should be made for responses in good and inclement weather as well as for workday, after-hours, and holiday responses.

There are no required minimum deployment times.

Requirements for Organization

Now you will learn about the communications requirements in NUREG-0654.

Communications

NUREG-0654 states:

- "Each organization shall establish reliable primary and backup means of communications . . . including provision for communicating between...state and local emergency operations centers, and radiological monitoring teams."
- "Conduct periodic testing of the communications system."
- "Communications drills between EOCs and field assessment teams shall be conducted at least annually."

According to the FEMA REP Program Manual, April 2012, field teams and their command post must have access to one communication system that is independent from the commercial telephone system.

Field teams must be able to report the radiological data they have collected to the field team coordinator promptly.

Requirements for Organization

Now you will learn about the requirements to have monitoring capabilities in NUREG-0654.

Monitoring Capabilities (1 of 2)

NUREG-0654 states:

- "Each organization . . . shall provide for offsite radiological monitoring equipment in the vicinity of the nuclear facility."
- "[There shall be] provisions to inspect, inventory, and operationally check equipment at least once each calendar quarter and after each use. There shall be sufficient reserves of equipment to replace those removed for calibration or repair. Calibration shall be at the interval recommended by the manufacturer."

Determining the presence of radioiodines and particulates during the early phase requires that air samples be taken and analyzed. Direct radiation measurements alone cannot differentiate between external exposure from the noble gases (xenon and krypton), iodines, and particulates. Nor would they be practical in determining the internal dose due to inhalation of iodines and particulates. Therefore, both instrumentation measuring gamma exposure rate and air sampling equipment are essential for verifying plume exposure rate.

Monitoring Capabilities (2 of 2)

During the intermediate phase, gamma exposure rate instruments are used to determine the boundaries of the restricted zone, the area within which persons who have not already been evacuated must be relocated. Air sampling equipment is used to determine whether resuspension of deposited radioactive material contributes significantly to dose.

All equipment used for this monitoring must be calibrated, and sufficient reserves of such equipment must be available to replace equipment that breaks or wears out during the heavy use to which it will be subjected. The FRMAC manuals describe the resources available for the Federal response as well as the quality assurance procedures and monitoring techniques used by the Federal response team.

In the next section of this lesson, you will learn more about types of monitoring equipment.

Survey Meters (1 of 5)

Properly calibrated low-range and high-range survey instruments are necessary for direct-exposure measurements during the early phase of the incident.

Low-range Geiger-Mueller (GM) or sealed ion chamber instruments have moveable beta shields that provide open and closed-window measurement capabilities. Readings with the beta window closed yield a gamma-only exposure rate, whereas readings with the window open yield a beta plus gamma exposure rate.

Open-window (beta plus gamma) readings taken at about one meter off the ground and near the ground that significantly exceed closed-window (gamma only) readings indicate that the operator is immersed in the plume. Taking an air sample at that location is warranted.

Open-window (beta plus gamma) readings significantly greater than closed-window (gamma only) readings only near the ground indicate groundshine, and the absence of a significant difference between open and closed-window readings indicates plume shine. In neither of these cases is taking an air sample warranted.

Survey Meters (2 of 5)

During the intermediate phase, gamma exposure rate instruments along with isotopic analysis of the deposited radionuclides are used to determine the boundaries of the restricted zone, the area within which persons who have not already been evacuated must be relocated. Air sampling equipment is used to determine whether resuspension of deposited radioactive material contributes significantly to dose.

All equipment used for this monitoring must be calibrated, and sufficient reserves of such equipment must be available to replace equipment that breaks or wears out during the heavy use to which it will be subjected. The FRMAC manuals describe the resources available for the Federal response as well as the quality assurance procedures and monitoring techniques used by the Federal response team.

Survey Meters (3 of 5)

GM instruments designed for measuring low exposure rates, e.g., tens of mR/hr, may malfunction at high exposure rates, e.g., tens of R/hr, because they become saturated. It is therefore important that a monitoring system include a high-range instrument or instruments capable of measuring higher gamma radiation exposure rates.

Survey Meters (4 of 5)

The time it takes for the positive ion sheath to reach the critical radius is called dead time. After the positive sheath passes the critical radius and moves on toward the cathode, the ionizations become stronger. The time it takes for the positive sheath to move from the critical radius to the cathode is called the recovery time.

Survey Meters (5 of 5)

The ionization pulse (electrical signal) generated must be of sufficient energy to be "seen" by the detector, which does not count anything below this minimum energy. If a GM detector is taken into an intense radiation field, any radiation penetrating the detector during the dead-time period is not counted. Any radiation interacting with the gas during the recovery time period is also not counted and prevents the detector from fully recovering. This effect is called saturation. In such a situation, the instrument will indicate essentially that background levels of radiation are present, when in fact the operator is in a high-radiation area. This is potentially a very serious situation and is the reason why low-range GM instruments must be accompanied by high-range survey meters during accident conditions.

Intermediate-phase operations may require the use of microR meters in addition to the mR and R meters discussed above. The derived response level equal to the 2-rem first-year relocation PAG may be in the tens to hundreds of µR/hr. Most microR meters are inorganic scintillation detectors such as 1

" x 1" sodium iodide, thallium-activated detectors [NaI(Tl)]. These instruments are expensive and may be damaged by careless handling. Care should be taken not to damage them while they are in use.

Air Sampler (1 of 2)

An air sampler is a calibrated air pump with the appropriate particulate filter and cartridge type absorber filter for selective collection of radioiodine in the presence of noble gases. Air samplers may be battery-powered or AC-supplied.

When an air sampler is in use, air flows first through the prefilter, trapping particulates such as cesium and up to 10% of the iodines available. The remaining iodines and noble gases (xenon and krypton) pass through the prefilter and enter the cartridge absorber, where the iodines are collected. The noble gases are then exhausted through the other end of the air sampler.

Air Sampler (2 of 2)

One of the most important aspects of early-phase air monitoring is selecting the appropriate sample collection media. Media considerations include:

- **Absorption** - A high efficiency particulate air (HEPA)–type prefilter placed before an absorber type filter medium cartridge can effectively separate the airborne radioactivity into iodine and particulate fractions. Using an appropriate inorganic absorber medium can reduce adsorption of fission product noble gases relative to radioiodine.
- **Charcoal** - Activated charcoal, an organic absorber media, efficiently collects radioiodine, but it also collects a significant portion of the radioactive noble gases. This property makes the charcoal absorber medium unacceptable for use with simple-operating gross radiation measurement instrumentation. (Charcoal may be used in practice exercises as long as silver media is available for actual emergency use.)

  If charcoal is to be used, Triethylene diamine (TEDA)–impregnated cartridges are recommended. TEDA acts as a chelating agent to chemically bind the iodines in the cartridge and reduce desorption loss.

- **Inorganic absorber media** - The three commercially available types of inorganic adsorber media are silver zeolite, silver silica gel, and silver alumina. Silver zeolite and silver alumina have higher rejection efficiency for noble gases (that is, they let noble gases go through them) and higher radioiodine retention efficiency (that is, they trap and hold iodine). Silver silica gel is in an activated, dry form, and its retention efficiency is reduced if used in high relative humidity.

Air Sample Media Analyzing System

According to NUREG-0654, each organization "shall have a capability to detect and measure radioiodine concentrations in air in the plume exposure EPZ as low as 10–7 µCi/cc under field conditions. Interference from the presence of noble gas and background radiation shall not decrease the stated minimum detectable activity."

Prior to removal of the air sample media from the air sampler, samples can be purged with uncontaminated air to remove noble gases left in the interstitial spaces of the cartridge when the air sampler was turned off. This purge is not required but it should not impact the time needed to obtain sample results significantly. This can easily be accomplished by immediately relocating to a low-background area outside of the plume upon completion of air sampling and energizing the air sampler for an additional five seconds.

A thin-window (1.5–2.0 mg/cm2) pancake GM detector or a 1" x 1" or 2" x 2" NaI(Tl) detector, with either a single-channel or dual-channel analyzer, may be used to measure the radioiodine activity on the absorber cartridge.

Air Sample System Limitations

Portable NaI(Tl) detector systems have some limitations. The more complex (dual-channel analyzer) system does not necessarily provide a more sensitive means of measuring the quantity of I-131 contained in the absorber medium than the simpler (single-channel) model.

Additionally, the smaller NaI(Tl) detectors do not have as good a spectral response as the larger laboratory detectors due to lower resolution and much lower peak–to–Compton continuum ratios.

A small NaI(Tl) system, with the threshold and window discriminators selected for the I-131 photopeak energy (364.48 keV), will include a significant number of counts due to the presence of other high-energy, short-lived isotopes of radioiodine (I-132, 133, 134, and 135).

Because of this effect, users of NaI(Tl) systems should develop detector response curves for absorber medium cartridges counted at varying times after reactor shutdown or use time-corrected dose conversion factors in dose projection calculations.

Example Air Sample

An airborne release may contain a complex mix of radionuclides.

A laboratory receiving samples to analyze must be capable of analyzing samples that contain a complex mix of radionuclides. The sampling time and date must be well documented on the sample.

Most air sampling systems should be able to meet the minimum detectable concentration requirement of 1x10–7 µCi/cc radioiodines. The calculations that should be carried out to ensure a particular system is in compliance with this standard are explained in Lesson 13.

Environmental Sampling Equipment (1 of 2)

Environmental sampling will take place in the intermediate phase of the accident. Many teams will be needed, and each team must be supplied with the appropriate sampling equipment. It is important to prevent cross-contamination of samples, so much of the sampling effort will involve contamination management.

For each type of sample taken (milk, soil, etc.), procedures should be in place establishing how to collect that particular type of sample. Chain-of-custody records must accompany each sample from the time the sample is collected until it reaches the laboratory. The methods used for sampling and for preserving chain of custody should be comparable to those discussed in the FRMAC manuals.

Environmental Sampling Equipment (2 of 2)

The FRMAC manuals describe, in detail, procedures that the Federal teams responding to an incident will employ in collecting environmental samples. These procedures designate the size of the sample to be collected, techniques employed, sample containers to be used, labeling, and chain of custody.

Milk Sample Kits

Milk sample kits from the EPA contain ion exchange method equipment. A new ion exchange cartridge must be used for each milk sample taken, and the funnel must be decontaminated after each use to prevent sample cross-contamination.

Personnel involved in sample taking must be trained in the sample collection procedures to be used and should participate in the six-year-cycle 50-mile Ingestion EPZ exercise. Equipment needed must be available for rapid deployment, exist in quantities appropriate for the accident and be inventoried quarterly.

Milk sampling can be accomplished either by taking a liquid sample or by passing the milk sample through an ion exchange resin. If the laboratory that is going to count the sample would require shipping, the ion exchange method might be the best option.

Requirements for Organization

Now that you have learned about the different types of monitoring equipment, you will learn about the training requirements in NUREG-0654.

Training Requirements (1 of 2)

NUREG-0654 states:

- "Radiological monitoring drills shall be conducted annually, including collection and analysis of all sample media (e.g. water, vegetation, soil, and air), and provisions for communications and record keeping."
- "Health physics drills shall be conducted semi-annually which involve response to, and analysis of, simulated airborne and liquid samples and direct radiation measurements in the environment."
- "[Each organization shall] participate in training."
- "Training and periodic retraining programs shall include radiological monitoring and analysis personnel."
- "Each organization shall provide for initial and annual retraining."

Training Requirements (2 of 2)

Having the equipment available is one thing; having personnel who know how to use it is another. NUREG-0654 requires that field monitoring personnel receive continuing training. Guidance Memorandum "Periodic Requirements–1" (GM PR-1) requires the state to send certification to FEMA annually documenting that personnel have received appropriate training in the operation of any equipment that they must use in the performance of their jobs.

FEMA's Office of General Counsel advises that "compliance with NUREG-0654/FEMA REP-1, Rev. 1 is not necessarily equivalent to compliance with the OSHA standard, nor does compliance with NUREG-0654/FEMA REP-1, Rev. 1 excuse compliance with 29 CFR 1910.120, if applicable."

The Occupational Safety and Health Administration (OSHA) requires that employers train their employees in proper procedures to safeguard their health. Requirements are defined in 29 CFR 1910.120, also known as the HAZWOPER (HAZardous Waste OPerations and Emergency Response) regulations. States are advised to consult their respective attorneys general to determine the applicability of the HAZWOPER regulations in their specific case.

Radiation Protection

You have now learned about field monitoring and its organization, including team composition, notification, deployment, communications, instrumentation, and training requirements.

Another important element of field monitoring is ensuring that workers are protected from radiation in the field. In the next section of this lesson, you will learn about radiation protection for field monitoring.

Dosimetry

NUREG-0654 requires "24-hour-per-day capability to determine the doses received by emergency personnel involved in any nuclear accident, including volunteers. Each organization shall make provisions for distribution of dosimeters, both self-reading and permanent record devices."

Emergency workers use direct-reading dosimeters to keep track of external exposure accrued during the incident and to ensure that they remain within administrative dose limits. Permanent, or more correctly, non-self-reading dosimeters serve as a more precise, legal record of dose; however, they must be processed in a laboratory to determine the dose received.

Electronic Personal Dosimeters

NUREG-0654 includes provisions to ensure that "dosimeters are read at appropriate frequencies and provide for maintaining dose records."

Many jurisdictions are now using electronic personal dosimeters with a range of 0–9,999 mR. Most, if not all, of the personal reading dosimeters (PRDs) have alarms which can be set to exposure limits. This type of dosimeter is easier to use and will eliminate potential problems. Regardless of what dosimeter is used, it must be read at regular intervals to prevent exceeding dose limits. Plans and procedures should specify the required interval at which these readings must be taken.

Non-Direct Reading Dosimetry

The two most common types of non-self-reading dosimeters are:

- **Optically stimulated luminescence technology dosimeter (OSLD) -** An optically stimulated luminescence technology dosimeter (OSLD) uses an Al2O3 crystal. The crystal structure changes when exposed to radiation. The amount of radiation exposure is measured by stimulating the Al2O3 material with green light. The resulting blue light emitted from the Al2O3 is proportional to the amount of radiation exposure. Many jurisdictions have opted to use OSLDs as their permanent record dosimeter.

- **Thermoluminescent dosimeter (TLD) -** A thermoluminescent dosimeter (TLD) is made of a material, such as lithium fluoride (LiF), that, when exposed to radiation, absorbs the energy from the radiation and transfers it to electrons of the phosphor atoms, which remain in an excited state. When the phosphor is heated, the electrons returning to their lower energy state emit light photons. The amount of light emitted is measured and corresponds directly to the amount of radiation to which the dosimeter has been exposed.

Regardless of which type is used, the dosimeter should be read by a processor accredited by the National Voluntary Laboratory Accreditation Program (NVLAP) or other accreditation program in accordance with ANSI standard N13.11-1983.

Respiratory Protection

Because of its many disadvantages, FEMA does not recommend that respiratory protection be used by state and local personnel responding as emergency workers for off-site missions involving nuclear power plant accidents. Respiratory protection can be effective in preventing inhalation of radioactive material and can take the form of:

- Air purifying respirators: Full-face and half-face masks containing filters
- Air-line respirators: Full-face and half-face masks attached by hose-line to a tank of air at a remote location
- Self-contained Breathing Apparatus: Full-face mask attached to a tank of air carried on person's back

Different types of respiratory protection offer varying levels of protection, measured by inhalation protection factors (PFs). The ambient air concentration of a contaminant in a particular environment divided by the PF of the equipment used will yield the concentration of the contaminant inhaled. For example, if the ambient air concentration of a contaminant is 500 ppm and the respirator used has a PF of 50, the inhaled concentration will be 10 ppm. Air-purifying masks range from in PF from 10 to 50, air-line respirators from 5 to 2,000, and SCBAs as high as 10,000.

Although it provides obvious advantages, respiratory protection also has some drawbacks, including limited air supply (SCBA), visual obstructions (full-face mask), physical stresses of wearing respiratory protection and larger external dose to the wearer due to slower task performance while wearing mask. Each worker who uses respiratory protection must meet the OSHA requirements.

Protective Clothing

Protective clothing, such as one-piece coveralls, limits skin contamination and may reduce beta skin dose. Protective clothing does not protect the wearer from gamma exposure.

Protective clothing may be of the disposable or launderable variety. Whichever type is used, provision must be made for replacement clothing once the teams report to decontamination.

During the intermediate phase, teams may take samples in areas where the public has not been evacuated or relocated. It may be beneficial for any protective clothing worn by these teams to be of a "non–nuclear emergency design" so as not to unduly alarm the public. Conventional work coveralls, rubber boots, and work gloves should serve for contamination management purposes as well as allowing the worker to remain relatively inconspicuous.

Potassium Iodide (KI)

NUREG-0654 requires that each organization make "provision for the use of radioprotective drugs and designate the method by which decision for administering radioprotective drug [will be] made."

Stable iodine, where appropriate, may be used as a prophylaxis to reduce thyroid dose from inhalation of radioiodines. Iodine doses to all workers during emergencies should be managed as described in the EPA's PAG Manual. Because of the slight possibility of an allergic reaction to the iodine, emergency workers should be checked for iodine sensitivity before it is administered. For further information about KI, review Lesson 8.

Decontamination

NUREG-0654 states that each organization shall "establish the means for radiological decontamination of personnel and equipment."

A worker's external exposure does not end until external decontamination is completed. The equipment used by monitoring teams must also be decontaminated, both in the field after each sample is taken, to prevent cross-contamination, and upon conclusion of operations as well.

Lesson Summary

In this lesson, you learned about field monitoring teams, how they are organized, and the measures taken to protect them from radiation. Let's summarize what you have learned in this lesson:

- Field teams: To constitute a field monitoring team, a team must have at least two personnel.
- Means of notification: Each organization must have in place a 24 hour system to communicate emergency events.
- Communications: Field teams must have a backup means of communication that does not rely on the commercial system.
- Monitoring equipment: Survey meters, air samplers, and other equipment must be regularly calibrated.
- Dosimetry: Dosimeters must be used to record personal doses for emergency workers.
- Managing Dose: Respiratory protection, protective clothing, potassium iodide, and other methods may be necessary to protect emergency works and other critical workers from radiation.

The next lesson will cover field monitoring operations.

Lesson 11: Field Monitoring Operations

Lesson Overview

In the previous lesson, you learned about the organization of field monitoring teams. In this lesson, you will learn about how field monitoring teams operate throughout the different phases of an incident.

Upon completion of this lesson, you will be able to:

- Explain the functions of field monitoring in radiological accident assessment.
- Identify sampling techniques, establish sampling priorities, and make personnel deployment decisions for collecting field samples and data during the early and intermediate phases of an incident.
- Describe the resources and tools used for data analysis during the early and intermediate phases that guide the decision making process.

Remember you can access the glossary in one of two ways throughout this course. You can select the glossary button in the top right hand corner of each main content screen. In addition, on content screens you can select underlined words to access their definitions in the online glossary. Selecting an underlined word will take you directly to its definition in the glossary.

This lesson should take approximately **45 minutes** to complete.

Field Monitoring Operations: Early Phase

As you have learned in previous lessons, an incident can be divided into three incident phases: early (emergency or plume), intermediate (post-plume, ingestion or relocation) and late (recovery). Some aspects of field monitoring are applicable only to the early phase, some only to the intermediate phase, and others are common to all the phases. Incident phases are identified in this lesson as they pertain to applicable field monitoring team functions, operations, and data analysis. Requirements are quoted from Nuclear Regulatory Commission Regulation (NUREG-0654), unless otherwise specified.

In this lesson, you will learn about the functions, operations, and data analysis of field monitoring during the early and intermediate phase. You will begin by learning about early phase functions, operations, and data analysis.

Functions of Early Phase Field Monitoring Teams

The primary purpose of plume exposure rate verification is to provide a flexible means of correcting, verifying and expanding on initial, inaccurate dose projections. The functions of early phase field monitoring teams include:

- Defining the plume (locating the perimeter of the radioactive cloud as it moves downwind).
- Verifying projections. Local meteorological or topographical conditions, such as coastal effects, river meander, building wake and precipitation may cause the off-site radioactive plume to behave differently from the projections made early in the accident. Field monitoring is therefore required to verify these projections.

- Collecting environmental measurements and verifying that actions taken based on projected concentrations are adequate to limit radiation exposure to members of the public. Are the protective actions in place adequate? Are the correct geographic areas protected?
- Indicating the need for further actions.
- Determining when protective actions should be terminated after the release of radioactive materials has stopped. When has the plume departed? When can those sheltering-in-place leave shelter?

Data Needed for Field Monitoring Teams

In order to dispatch teams to the appropriate locations for monitoring, field monitoring team coordinators need to be aware of:

- Wind direction: Where is the release going?
- Wind speed: How fast will it get there?
- Atmospheric stability class: What amount of dispersion is taking place?
- Meteorological and topographic conditions that may influence the transport of the plume, such as river valleys, coastlines, mountains, precipitation, and approaching fronts: What will affect the downwind concentrations?

 Additionally, information about plant conditions and release composition is important. The type of release (normal coolant, gap, core melt, vessel melt-through) and containment hold-up time (which allows for a delay) significantly affect the radionuclide mix in the effluent and the potential dose. Releases containing radioiodines influence the decision on whether to administer potassium iodide. The release of certain particulates may require assigning extremely low dosimeter limits to control internal dose.

Plume-Projected Dose Verification

 The plume-projected dose is verified by first traversing the plume and making the following readings:

- While traversing, determine edge and centerline (closed window)
- At centerline, at both waist and ground level:
    - Gamma only (closed window)
    - Gamma and beta (open window)

Beta plus gamma values significantly in excess of the gamma only values indicate the presence of the radioactive nuclides that are the constituents of the plume. When such values are encountered, the plume is surrounding the team. This is called immersion. When the presence of the plume is verified, air sampling for radioiodine and particulates is warranted.

Plume Direction Projections

The state, utility, NRC, and DOE may provide plume pathway projections in the incident's early phase. There are several models for projecting plume direction.

- **Straight-Line Gaussian -** The straight-line Gaussian projection model is a relatively simple plume diffusion projection. It is frequently used because it is both fast and easy. It also makes a lot of assumptions and does not take into consideration changes in wind direction downwind from the release point.

- **Variable Trajectory** - NARAC is an atmospheric modeling system based at Lawrence Livermore National Laboratory. NARAC can predict the atmospheric diffusion of a plume as influenced by local meteorological and topographical conditions using a suite of computer codes and models.

NARAC advisories may consist of predicted concentration patterns, estimated exposure rate patterns, dose projections and predicted ingestion pathway concentrations.

The Aerial Measuring System (AMS) is an aerial radiation surveillance program operated for the Department of Energy. Using both fixed-wing and rotary aircraft, AMS can conduct aerial surveys of deposited materials after the plume has dissipated.

A lead time of 12 hours is desired when aerial measurements are requested. Since it is not necessary to begin foodstuff monitoring for 36 to 48 hours after a release, AMS could survey the area surrounding the site prior to sampling. This would allow authorities to concentrate the initial sampling effort in areas where greatest radioiodine deposition has occurred.

Lesson 11: Field Monitoring Operations

Every state has a designated radiological laboratory for use in nuclear incidents. The laboratory should be certified and have proper instrument calibrations. Usually, the laboratories selected are analytical laboratories that do routine environmental analysis.

During the early phase of the accident, particulate filters and iodine sample cartridges are sent to the lab. They may be many more times radioactive than the samples the lab usually handles. Procedures for handling these "hot" samples should be in place. Particulate filters should receive expedited analysis, as information about the mix will prove valuable during the intermediate phase.

Field Monitoring Operations: Intermediate Phase

Now that you have learned about the functions, operations, and data analysis of field monitoring during the early phase, you will learn about the functions, operations, and data analysis of field monitoring during the intermediate phase.

Functions of Intermediate Phase Field Monitoring Teams (1 of 2)

The initial decisions made during the early phase of a nuclear power plant accident are based on plant conditions and projections. During the intermediate phase, however, "real" data (i.e., field environmental measurements) can be gathered for use in assessing the situation accurately and implementing appropriate protective actions.

The goal of field monitoring teams during the intermediate phase includes environmental sampling to obtain data upon which to base decisions regarding:

- The ingestion pathway with an emphasis on crops near harvest: What are the contamination levels? Are contamination levels lower than acceptable standards? Can it be proven that there is no contamination?
- Relocation and reentry: Do the restricted zone boundaries need to be expanded or relaxed? Is relocation temporary or permanent in a particular area? If temporary, when may people return to their residences?
- Adjustment of protective action decisions (PADs): The actual path of the plume as established by measurements is likely to be quite different from that predicted with dispersion calculations. Sampling can determine whether areas bounded by the early-phase protective actions must be expanded or contracted.

Functions of Intermediate Phase Field Monitoring Teams (2 of 2)

Another priority during the intermediate phase is determining whether there are "hot spots." This is particularly important if there are areas measured greater than 10 mR/hr because of the 96 hours of exposure that is included in the plume (exposure) phase protective action guides (PAGs) calculations.

Depending on the nuclides that are producing the measured 10 mR/hr (or greater), any population not already evacuated warrants being evacuated based on exceeding the plume phase PAG even though the incident may have advanced to the intermediate phase.

Other priorities during the intermediate phase include determining:

- Where evacuated residents may safely return
- Areas where reentry must be limited
- Areas where decontamination activities must be conducted on exit of the reentry areas

Determining Sampling Locations

Information needed for determining appropriate sampling locations during the intermediate phase include:

- Early phase field monitoring team data: The areas where early phase measurements were obtained and would lead to the expectations of intermediate need samples.
- Source term: The particular type or amount of radionuclides originating at the source of a nuclear accident. The source term will vary depending upon the type of accident.
- Plant conditions: Indications of the source term's contents and duration of the release.
- Meteorology: Were there dispersion conditions? Was there precipitation that might increase ground concentrations? Did wind shifts occur during the release?
- Early-phase data: Laboratory analysis of iodine samples and particulate filters should be available.
- Projections: State and/or utility as well as Nuclear Regulatory Commission (NRC) projections should be available. The DOE will provide a National Atmospheric Release Advisory Capability (NARAC) projection for a serious accident.

Land Use Data

In addition to the data that you just learned about that can help determine appropriate sampling locations, land use data is also critical to prioritizing sampling locations.

The local emergency response plan generally does not include land use data because the data are constantly changing. These data are often available from the local county extension agency or other state agricultural agency. The emergency response plan should, however, note the location of a land use database.

Harvesting Data

In addition to land use data, current harvesting data is also critical to prioritizing sampling locations.

Farmers have a narrow window for harvesting crops. If an accident occurs, the crops that would be harvested within the next 30 days should be determined, and the appropriate lists of farms growing those crops and the emergency planning zone (EPZ) map showing their locations would be used to develop the monitoring plan. Sampling of these crops would be a priority since the potential loss of a crop is a critical economic issue for local farmers

Data Analysis

During the early phase, field monitoring teams will have taken air samples. The particulate filters should have undergone laboratory analysis and should have received expedited handling.

In the intermediate phase, the results of this analysis provide the first indication of the nuclide mix involved with the deposition.

Next, you will learn about milk sampling techniques used to gather further data and how contamination control is applied to samples in the intermediate phase.

Sampling Techniques

You learned about milk sample ion exchange equipment in Lesson 10. The ion exchange method involves passing a 3–4 liter sample of contaminated milk through a column of anion resin to collect the iodines present in the sample. The anion resin is the chloride form of a strongly basic ion exchanger. The iodines are retained within the resin column for analysis.

Calibration curves for the appropriate instrument system (that have been developed prior to the accident) are used to determine the activity present in the milk. The milk activity is then compared to the U.S. Food and Drug Administration (FDA) derived intervention levels (DILs) to provide a basis for determining appropriate protective actions.

Contamination Control

Field teams should employ the following techniques to prevent cross-contamination of samples and to ensure integrity of data.

- **Best practices** - All samples should be double-bagged. All sampling equipment used at a sample collection site should be decontaminated before reusing at another sampling location. Teams sampling in "cold" areas should not be sent to areas of suspected high activity.
- **Representative sample** - If deposition appears to be relatively even, fewer samples need to be taken. A high degree of variation requires more samples.
- **Labels** - All monitoring personnel should be trained to use the same system for identification of samples and data collection. The identification should be attached to all sample containers at the time of collection and should include the following information:
    - Date
    - Time
    - Type of sample (grass, soil, milk, etc.)
    - Location of sample collection point
    - Area represented by the sample
    - Identity of person or team collecting the sample
- **"Hot line"** - All samples should be accounted for and rebagged at a control line. This line, also called the "hot line," is designed to separate contaminated and noncontaminated areas.

Data Evaluation

Data evaluation in the intermediate phase yields:

- DILs: Calculated radionuclide concentrations in foodstuffs, milk and water, which, if ingested without any protective actions, would result in a projected dose commitment equivalent to the FDA PAGs.
- Buildup curves: Provide a basis for comparing milk measurements from samples taken at various times following the initial ingestion.
- Nuclide mix: The specific isotopes deposited from the particular accident.

Laboratory Use

Because of the high number of samples taken during the intermediate phase, samples are contaminated and minimum detectable levels are different from those in the materials the laboratories normally handle. Laboratories will continue to be working outside of routine conditions. Adequate planning, written procedures and training are essential for effective sampling and laboratory analysis during this phase.

Lesson Summary

Let's summarize what you learned in this lesson:

- Early Phase
    - Field monitoring team functions to define plume, verify projections, collect environmental measurements, and determine further actions.
    - The plume-projected dose is verified.
    - Plume pathway projection is provided by the state, utility, NRC, and DOE, using either straight-line Gaussian or variable trajectory models.
- Intermediate Phase

- o   Function of field monitoring in this phase is to gather the data that will be used to accurately assess the situation and take appropriate actions.
- o   Contamination and sampling techniques are applied.
- o   Data is evaluated and yields DILs, buildup curves, nuclide mix, and summation of partial PAGs.

Lesson 12: Introduction to SI Units

Lesson Overview

The purpose of this module is to review the relationship between the International System of Units and the customary units for radiological measurement.

Upon completion of this lesson, you will be able to:

- Describe the relationships between the International System of Units (SI Units) and the customary units for radiological measurements.
- Convert from SI to customary units and customary units to SI using a hand calculator.

Remember you can access the glossary in one of two ways throughout this course. You can select the glossary button in the top right hand corner of each main content screen. In addition, on content screens you can select underlined words to access their definitions in the online glossary. Selecting an underlined word will take you directly to its definition in the glossary.

This lesson should take approximately **1 hour** to complete.

Introduction to SI Units

The transition to measurement using the International System of Units, or SI, which stands for Systeme International d'Unites, is required by Presidential Executive Order 12770 and Public Laws 94-168 and 100-418.

To ensure a smooth transition to SI units, international and domestic organizations have begun showing information on packages and shipping documents in both the SI and customary units.

Many sources of information use customary units, such as the Curie, and others use SI units, such as the Becquerel. Going from one measurement to another requires the use of a conversion factor, which you'll learn more about later in this lesson.

Before moving on to measurement conversions, let's review the metric prefixes used to more easily express measured values.

Metric Prefixes

Since very large and very small numbers are used in quantifying radioactive materials, it is necessary to use numerical abbreviations to write the measured values in a practical way. The most common units used in measurements to describe radiation characteristics are:

- kilo (k) = 10 x 103
- milli (m) = 10 x 10-3
- micro (µ) = 10 x 10-6
- nano (n) = 10 x 10-9
- pico (p) = 10 x 10-12

Now that you understand metric prefixes, let's review common units of measure and learn their SI equivalents.

Radiological Units

- **Curie (Ci)** - The curie (Ci) describes the quantity or activity of radioactive materials. It is equal to 37 billion disintegrations per second (dps).

  Its SI equivalent, the becquerel (Bq), is equal to only 1 dps.
  Therefore:
    - 1 Bq = 27 pCi
    - 1 Ci = 37 GBq

- **Rad** - The amount of energy deposited in any material is measured in rads. The rad is the unit of absorbed dose. 1 rad = 100 ergs/gram.
  Its SI equivalent, the gray (Gy), is equal to 1 joule/kilogram.
  Therefore:
    - 1.) Gy = 100 rad

- **Rem** - The rem (roentgen equivalent man) is used to measure the dose equivalent to human tissue.
  Its SI equivalent is the sievert (Sv).
    - 2.) 1 Sv = 100 rem

Other Common Units

Many SI units are used in dose projections and accident assessments. The list below contains those most commonly used in this course.

- **Length** - The meter (m) is the SI unit of length. Common units of measure are equal to the following:
    - 1 inch (in) = 2.540 centimeters (cm)
    - 1 foot (ft) = 12 in = 30.48 cm (or 0.3048 m)
    - 1 yard (yd) = 0.9144 m • 1 mile (mi) = 5280 ft = 1.609 kilometers (km)
    - 1 km = 1000 m = 0.6214 mi

To quickly convert between miles (mi) and kilometers (km), use the following:

- ____ mi x 1.61 = ____ km
  - ____ km ÷ 1.61 = ____ mi

- **Velocity** - The SI unit of velocity is meters/second (m/sec). Common units of measure are equal to the following:
  - 1 mile per hour (mph) = 0.4469 m/sec (or 1.467 ft/sec = 1.609 km/h)
  - 1 knot (kt) = 1.151 mph
  - 1 m/sec = 3.281 ft/sec = 2.237 mph = 3.6 km/h
  To quickly convert between miles per hour (mph) and meters/second (m/sec), use the following:
  - ____ mph x 0.45 = ____ m/sec
  - ____ m/sec ÷ 0.45 = ____ mph
- **Area** - The SI unit of area is the square meter (m2). Common units of measure are equal to the following:
  - 1 in2 = 6.452 cm2
  - 1 ft2 = 144 in2 = 929.0 cm2
  - 1 yd2 = 0.836 m2
  - 1 mi2 = 2.59 km2
  Remember that:
  - 10,000 cm2 = 1 m2
- **Volume** - The SI unit of volume is the cubic meter (m3). Common units of measure are equal to the following:
  - 1 gal = 3.785 liters (l)
  - 1 in3 = 16.387 cm3 (cc)
  - 1 ft3 = 28.32 l
  Remember that:
  - 1,000,000 cm3 = 1 m3
- **Flow rate** – An SI unit of flow rate is liters per minute (lpm). 1 cubic foot per minute (cfm) is equal to 28.32 lpm.
  To quickly convert between cfm and lpm, use the following:
  - ____ cfm x 28.32 = ____ lpm
  - ____ lpm ÷ 28.32 = ____ cfm
- **Weight** - The SI unit of weight is the gram (g). Common units of measure are equal to the following:
  - 1 ounce (oz) = 28.32 grams (g)
  - 1 pound (lb) = 0.4536 kilograms (kg)
  To quickly convert between lbs and kg, use the following:
  - ____ lbs x 0.45 = ____ kg
  - ____ kg ÷ 0.45 = ____ lbs
- **Temperature**- The SI unit of temperature is the Kelvin (K). Common units of measure are equal to the following:
  - 0° Fahrenheit (F) = –17.778° Celsius (C)

- 1° C = 1.8° F
- 0° C = 273° Kelvin (K)

To convert Fahrenheit (F) to Kelvin (K), you must first convert Fahrenheit (F) to Celsius (C) as follows:

- °C = (°F − 32) ÷ 1.8
- °F = (1.8 x °C) + 32

Kelvin (K) is calculated with:

- °K = °C + 273

- **Density** - The SI unit of density is the kilogram per cubic meter (kg/m3). Common units of measure are equal to the following:
  - 0.03613 lb/in3 = 1 g/cm3
  - 62.43 lb/ft3 = 1000 kg/m3

- **Pressure** - The SI unit of pressure is the pascal (Pa). Common units of measure are equal to the following:
  - 1 atmosphere (atm) = 14.696 lb/in2 = 101.33 kiloPascals (kPa) = 760 mm mercury (Hg) = 29.92 in. Hg
  - 1 pound per square inch (psi) = 6.8947 kPa

Application

Now that you have learned about several important units of measure, you will learn how to perform unit analysis for simple and complex conversions, and how to calculate activity from detector readings.

Unit Analysis – Simple Conversions

Unit analysis is the process of converting from one unit to another.

For example, one millicurie of Cs-137 equals how many becquerels?

Locate the conversion factor or factors that will allow you to convert to the desired unit. In this example, the necessary conversion factors are 1000 millicuries equals 1 curie, 1 curie equals 3.7 times 10 to the 10th disintegrations per second, and 1 becquerel equals 1 disintegration per second.

The unit analysis can now be completed by substituting in the conversion factors and solving the equation.

1 millicurie is equal to 3.7 times 10 to the 7th becquerels.

Unit Analysis – Complex Conversions

The process of unit analysis using conversion factors is applied to complex conversions as well as simple ones. 8.63 times 10 to the negative 9th sievert per becquerel equals how many millirem per picocurie?

Locate the conversion factor or factors that will allow you to convert to the desired unit. In this example, the necessary conversion factors are as follows: 1 sievert equals 100 rem.

Since 1 rem is equal to 1000 millirem, you can find that 1 sievert is equal to 1 times 10 to the 5th millirem. 1 becquerel is equal to 1 disintegration per second.

1 curie is equal to 3.7 times 10 to the 10th disintegrations per second.

Since 1 curie is equal to 1 times 10 to the 12th picocurires, you can find that 1 times 10 to the 12th picocurires equals 3.7 times 10 to the 10th disintegrations per second.

The unit analysis can now be completed by substituting in the conversion factors and solving the equation.

8.63 times 10 to the negative 9th sievert per becquerel equals 3.19 times 10 to the negative 5th millirem per picocurie.

Detector Readings

This equation is used to calculate the activity from a detector reading.

"A" represents the activity, or decay rate, measured in microcuries. This equation will be used to solve for "A."

To find the activity, you'll need values for 'G,' 'B,' and efficiency.

The detector efficiency will vary based on the kind of the detector and the material being measured.

G represents the gross count, in counts per minute.

B represents the background count, also in counts per minute.

With those three values, the activity can be calculated. For example: given a detector efficiency of 10% for Cesium-137, an average background rate of 216 counts per minute in the absence of the sample, and a count of 25,306 counts per minute for the sample, what is the activity of the sample in microcuries?

All the values need to be substituted in.

Then it can be solved.

The activity sample is 0.11 microcuries.

Lesson Summary

Let's summarize what you have learned in this lesson:

- The transition to measurement using SI is required by Presidential Executive Order and Public Laws.

- Common units of measure have an SI equivalent: The SI equivalent of the Curie (Ci) is the Becquerel (Bq).
- The SI equivalent of the Rad is the Gray (Gy).
- The SI equivalent of the Rem is the Seivert (Sv).

The process of converting from one unit to another is called unit analysis. It is performed with the following steps: On the left side of the equation, place the unit you are converting from.

Locate the conversion factors that will allow you to convert to the desired unit.

Multiply the right side of the equation by the conversion factors.

The next lesson will provide an overview of mathematical equations used throughout the course and how to solve problems using the equations.

Lesson 13: Equations

Lesson Overview

In this lesson, you will explore the equations used throughout this course. Each equation is presented with an example problem and the solution.

Upon completion of this lesson, you will be able to:

- Identify and understand the different formulas used throughout the course.
- Accurately apply the correct formula to real-life situations.

This lesson should take approximately **1 hour** to complete.

Generalized Gaussian Equation for Ground Level Release, Downwind Centerline Value

This equation is used to calculate the concentration of radioactive material in the air directly downwind from a release that occurs at ground level.

Chi represents the concentration of curie per meter cubed. This equation will be used to solve for chi.

Note: curie per meter cubed is equivalent to micro-curie per centimeter cubed; chi can be expressed in either format.

This equation's purpose is to determine the concentration of radioactive material at different distances downwind from a ground-level release. The variable "x" represents the distance from the release, in meters, being measured.

Since the equation is measuring the concentration directly on the centerline, "y" is 0 in this equation.

Similarly, this equation measures the concentration at ground level, so "z," which is the meters above the surface being measured, is also 0.

The height of release for this equation is also 0, since it is a ground level release.

As you can observe, "x" doesn't appear in the equation itself. Rather, it will be used to find sigma-sub-y and sigma-sub-z.

Those values will be found using graphs which we'll explore soon.

The other values needed are "Q" and mu. "Q" is the release rate, measured in curies per second.

Mu represents wind speed at ground level, which is measured in meters per second.

Sigma-sub-y and sigma-sub-z are both values measured in meters. Determining their values requires the use of established resources.

This table and the following figures come from the EPA's Workbook of Atmospheric Dispersion Estimates, published in 1970. To make a more accurate dose projection, use this table to estimate the combined atmosphere and wind speed's stability class.

Once the stability class is determined, sigma-sub-y can be found using this figure. The log-log graph is read along the bottom out to a desired distance, up to the appropriate stability class line, then left to the sigma-sub-y value, in meters.

For example, at 5 kilometers downwind and a D stability, the sigma-sub-y is 300 meters.

Sigma-sub-z can be found using Figure 13-3. The value of sigma-sub-z is determined in the same manner as the value of sigma-sub-y.

Now back to the equation, all of the values necessary to find chi are available. For example: Given a release rate of 3 curies per second, on an overcast night, with a wind speed of 7 meters per second, what is the centerline concentration 3 kilometers from the release point?

Using Table 13-1, the neutral class D should be applied due to overcast conditions, which allows you to use Figure 13-2 to find sigma-sub-y: 190 meters.

Next use Figure 13-3 to find sigma-sub-z: 65 meters.

Now back to the equation, all the values need to be substituted in.

Then it can be solved.

The centerline concentration 3 kilometers downwind of the ground level release is 1.1 times 10 to the negative 5th curie per meter-cubed.

Generalized Gaussian Equation for Elevated Release, Downwind Centerline Value

This equation is used to calculate the concentration of radioactive material in the air directly downwind from a release that occurs at an elevated release.

Chi represents the concentration of curie per meter cubed, or micro-curie per centimeter cubed. This equation will be used to solve for chi.

This equation's purpose is to determine the concentration of radioactive material at different distances as it is released at different heights. The variable "x" represents the distance from the release, in meters.

This equation solves for chi at 0 meters from centerline and 0 meters above the surface.

The variable "H" represents the effective height of the release, in meters.

As you can observe, "x" doesn't appear in the equation itself. Rather, it will be used to find sigma-sub-y and sigma-sub-z. Those values will be found using graphs which we'll explore soon.

The other values needed are "Q" and mu. "Q" is the release rate, measured in curies per second. Mu represents wind speed at the release height, which is measured in meters per second.

Sigma-sub-y and sigma-sub-z are both values measured in meters. Determining their values requires the use of established resources.

This table and the following figures come from the EPA's Workbook of Atmospheric Dispersion Estimates, published in 1970. To make a more accurate dose projection, use this table to estimate the combined atmosphere and wind speed's stability class.

Once the stability class is determined, sigma-sub-y can be found using this figure. The log-log graph is read along the bottom out to a desired distance, up to the appropriate stability class line, then left to the sigma-sub-y value, in meters.

For example, at 5 kilometers downwind and a D stability, the sigma-sub-y is 300 meters.

Sigma-sub-z can be found using figure 13-3. The value of sigma-sub-z is determined in the same manner as the value of sigma-sub-y.

Now back to the equation, all of the values necessary to find chi are available. For example:

Given a release rate of 80 curies per second on an overcast morning, with a wind speed of 6 meters per second, and an effective release height of 60 meters, what is the centerline concentration 500 meters from the release point?

Using Table 13-1, the neutral class D should be applied due to overcast conditions, which allows you to use Figure 13-2 to find sigma-sub-y: 36 meters.

Next use figure 13-3 to find sigma-sub-z: 18.5 meters.

Now back to the equation, all the values need to be substituted in.

Then it can be solved.

The centerline concentration 500 meters downwind of an effective release height of 60 meters is 3.3 times 10 to the negative 5th curie per meter-cubed.

Generalized Gaussian Equation for Ground Level Release, Off-Centerline Value

This equation is used to calculate the concentration of radioactive material in the air at a location not directly downwind centerline after a ground level release.

Chi represents the concentration of curie per meter cubed, or micro-curie per centimeter cubed. This equation will be used to solve for chi.

This equation's purpose is to determine the concentration of radioactive material at different distances not directly downwind centerline from a ground level release. The variable "x" represents the distance from the release, in meters.

"y" is the distance from centerline, in meters.

"z," which is the meters above the surface being measured, is 0.

The height of release for this equation is also 0, since it is a ground level release.

As you can observe, "x" doesn't appear in the equation itself. Rather, it will be used to find sigma-sub-y and sigma-sub-z. Those values will be found using graphs which we'll explore soon.

The other values needed are "Q" and mu. "Q" is the release rate, measured in curies per second.

Mu represents wind speed at the release height, which is measured in meters per second.

Sigma-sub-y and sigma-sub-z are both values measured in meters. Determining their values requires the use of established resources.

This table and the following figures come from the EPA's Workbook of Atmospheric Dispersion Estimates, published in 1970. To make a more accurate dose projection, use this table to estimate the combined atmosphere and wind speed's stability class.

Once the stability class is determined, sigma-sub-y can be found using this figure. The log-log graph is read along the bottom out to a desired distance, up to the appropriate stability class line, then left to the sigma-sub-y value, in meters.

For example, at 5 kilometers downwind and a D stability, the sigma-sub-y is 300 meters.

Sigma-sub-z can be found using figure 13-3. The value of sigma-sub-z is determined in the same manner as the value of sigma-sub-y.

Now back to the equation, all of the values necessary to find chi are available. For example:

Given a release rate of 3 curies per second, on an overcast night, with a wind speed of 7 meters per second, what is the concentration 3 kilometers from the release point 500 meters off-center?

Using Table 13-1, the neutral class D should be applied due to overcast conditions.

which allows you to use Figure 13-2 to find sigma-sub-y: 190 meters.

Next use figure 13-3 to find sigma-sub-z: 65 meters.

Now back to the equation, all the values need to be substituted in.

Then it can be solved.

The concentration 3 kilometers from a release point, 500 meters off-center is 3.4 times 10 to the negative 7th curie per meter-cubed.

Calculating Off-Centerline Distance to a Desired Value from Centerline Value at a Specific Distance

A centerline concentration may have been determined by an air sample taken at a point downwind. From that concentration, an off-centerline concentration may be calculated.

"y" represents the distance from centerline, in meters. This equation will be used to find "y."

Note that "y" is the distance from the centerline. The plume width is 2 times y.

Two different values of chi, as well as sigma-sub-y, are needed to solve for "y."

The chi in the numerator represents the centerline concentration that has been taken at a point downwind.

The chi in the denominator is the concentration off-centerline.

Sigma-sub-y is a value measured in meters. Determining its value requires the use of established resources.

This table and the following figure come from the EPA's Workbook of Atmospheric Dispersion Estimates, published in 1970. To make a more accurate dose projection, use this table to estimate the combined atmosphere and wind speed's stability class.

Once the stability class is determined, sigma-sub-y can be found using this figure. The log-log graph is read along the bottom out to a desired distance, up to the appropriate stability class line, then left to the sigma-sub-y value, in meters.

For example, at 5 kilometers downwind and a D stability, the sigma-sub-y is 300 meters.

Back to the equation, all of the values necessary to find "y" are available. For example:

Given a downwind centerline concentration at 3 kilometers of 1.1 times 10 to the negative 5th curie per meter cubed, on an overcast morning, at what distance from centerline is the concentration of 3.48 times 10 to the negative 7th curie per meter cubed?

Using Table 13-1, the neutral class D should be applied due to overcast conditions.

which allows you to use Figure 13-2 to find sigma-sub-y: 190 meters.

Now back to the equation, all the values need to be substituted in.

Then it can be solved.

The distance from the centerline is 500 meters.

Remember that "y" is the distance from the centerline in either direction, which means the plume of the concentration chosen is 1,000 meters wide.

Generalized Gaussian Equation for Elevated Release, Off-Centerline Value

This equation is used to calculate the concentration of radioactive material in the air at a location not directly downwind centerline after an elevated release.

Chi represents the concentration of curie per meter cubed, or micro-curie per centimeter cubed. This equation will be used to solve for chi.

This equation's purpose is to determine the concentration of radioactive material at different distances as it is released at different heights. The variable "x" represents the distance from the release, in meters.

"y" is the distance from centerline, in meters.

"z," which is meters above the surface being measured, is 0.

The variable "H" represents the effective height of the release, in meters.

As you can observe, "x" doesn't appear in the equation itself. Rather, it will be used to find sigma-sub-y and sigma-sub-z. Those values will be found using graphs which we'll explore soon.

The other values needed are "Q" and mu. "Q" is the release rate, measured in curies per second.

Mu represents wind speed at the release height, which is measured in meters per second.

Sigma-sub-y and sigma-sub-z are both values measured in meters. Determining their values requires the use of established resources.

This table and the following figures come from the EPA's Workbook of Atmospheric Dispersion Estimates, published in 1970. To make a more accurate dose projection, use this table to estimate the combined atmosphere and wind speed's stability class.

Once the stability class is determined, sigma-sub-y can be found using this figure. The log-log graph is read along the bottom out to a desired distance, up to the appropriate stability class line, then left to the sigma-sub-y value, in meters.

For example, at 5 kilometers downwind and a D stability, the sigma-sub-y is 300 meters.

Sigma-sub-z can be found using figure 13-3. The value of sigma-sub-z is determined in the same manner as the value of sigma-sub-y.

Now back to the equation, all of the values necessary to find chi are available. For example:

Given a release rate of 80 curies per second on an overcast morning, with a wind speed of 6 meters per second, and an effective release height of 60 meters, at 500 meters downwind, what is the concentration 50 meters off-centerline?

Using Table 13-1, the neutral class D should be applied due to overcast conditions, which allows you to use Figure 13-2 to find sigma-sub-y: 36 meters.

Next use figure 13-3 to find sigma-sub-z: 18.5 meters.

Now back to the equation, all the values need to be substituted in.

Then it can be solved.

The concentration 50 meters off-centerline 500 meters downwind of an effective release height of 60 meters is 1.3 times 10 to the negative 5th curie per meter-cubed.

Fumigation (Atmospheric Mixing Lid)

 The mixing lid acts as a ceiling, keeping radioactive material concentrated near the surface. This equation can be used to determine the concentration of radioactive material in this instance.

Chi represents the concentration of curie per meter cubed, or microcurie per centimeter cubed. This equation will be used to solve for chi.

The variable "x" represents the distance from the release, in meters.

This equation solves for chi at 0 meters from centerline, 0 meters above the surface, and a 0-meter effective height of release.

As you can observe, "x" doesn't appear in the equation itself. Rather, it will be used to find sigma-sub-y. That value will be found using figures which we'll explore soon.

The other values needed to find chi are "Q," "L," and mu.

"Q" is the release rate, measured in curies per second.

"L" is the height of the lid, in meters.

Mu represents wind speed at effective release height, which is measured in meters per second.

Sigma-sub-y is measured in meters. Determining its value requires the use of established resources.

This table and the following figures come from the EPA's Workbook of Atmospheric Dispersion Estimates, published in 1970. To make a more accurate dose projection, use this table to estimate the combined atmosphere and wind speed's stability class.

Once the stability class is determined, sigma-sub-y can be found using this figure. The log-log graph is read along the bottom out to a desired distance, up to the appropriate stability class line, then left to the sigma-sub-y value, in meters.

For example, at 5 kilometers downwind and a D stability, the sigma-sub-y is 300 meters.

With that information, the concentration under a lid can be determined. For example:

Given a release rate of 10 curies per second, on an overcast night, a wind speed of 7 meters per second, and the lid at 500 meters, what is the centerline concentration at 5 kilometers?

Using Table 13-1, the neutral class D should be applied due to overcast conditions, which allows you to use Figure 13-2 to find sigma-sub-y: 300 meters.

Now back to the equation, all the values need to be substituted in.

Then it can be solved.

The centerline concentration at 5 kilometers is 3.8 times 10 to the negative 6th curie per meter cubed.

Building Wake

Large structures at the release point alter the dispersion of radioactive material. The effect washes out at 1 to 2 miles, or 2 to 3 kilometers. This equation is used to calculate the concentration of radioactive material in the air directly downwind from a release that occurs at ground level with a building altering the dispersion.

Chi represents the concentration of curie per meter cubed, or micro-curie per centimeter cubed. This equation will be used to solve for chi.

This equation's purpose is to determine the concentration of radioactive material at different distances as it is affected by the wake of large structures. The variable "x" represents the distance from the release, in meters.

This equation solves for chi at 0 meters from centerline, 0 meters above the surface, and a 0-meter effective height of release.

As you can observe, "x" doesn't appear in the equation itself. Rather, it will be used to find sigma-sub-y and sigma-sub-z. Those values will be found using graphs which we'll explore soon.

The other values needed are "Q," mu, "c" and "A." "Q" is the release rate, measured in curies per second.

Mu represents wind speed at ground level, which is measured in meters per second.

"c" is the shape factor, which is usually zero point five (typical building shape).

"A" is the cross-sectional area in meters squared. This is equal to the building's height multiplied by width.

Sigma-sub-y and sigma-sub-z are both values measured in meters. Determining their values requires the use of established resources.

This table and the following figures come from the EPA's Workbook of Atmospheric Dispersion Estimates, published in 1970. To make a more accurate dose projection, use this table to estimate the combined atmosphere and wind speed's stability class.

Once the stability class is determined, sigma-sub-y can be found using this figure. The log-log graph is read along the bottom out to a desired distance, up to the appropriate stability class line, then left to the sigma-sub-y value, in meters.

For example, at 5 kilometers downwind and a D stability, the sigma-sub-y is 300 meters.

Sigma-sub-z can be found using figure 13-3. The value of sigma-sub-z is determined in the same manner as the value of sigma-sub-y.

Now back to the equation, all of the values necessary to find chi are available. For example: given a release rate of 10 curies per second, on an overcast day, with a wind speed of 7 meters per second, and a containment building 75 meters tall and 50 meters wide, which yields a cross-sectional area of 3750 meters squared, what is the concentration at 1 kilometer?

Using Table 13-1, the neutral class D should be applied due to overcast conditions, which allows you to use Figure 13-2 to find sigma-sub-y: 70 meters.

Next use Figure 13-3 to find sigma-sub-z: 32 meters.

Now back to the equation, all the values need to be substituted in.

Then it can be solved.

The concentration at 1 kilometer is 1.6 times 10 to the negative 4th curie per meter cubed.

Volumetric Diffusion

Radioactive material will remain concentrated while traveling up or down a valley unless there is a strong crosswind. This equation can be used to determine the concentration of radioactive material as it moves along a valley.

Chi represents the concentration of curie per meter cubed, or micro-curie per centimeter cubed. This equation will be used to solve for chi.

The variable "x" represents the distance from the release, in meters.

This equation solves for chi at 0 meters from centerline, 0 meters above the surface, and a 0-meter effective height of release.

The values needed to find chi are "Q," mu, "H" and "W."

"Q" is the release rate, measured in curies per second.

Mu represents wind speed at the release height, which is measured in meters per second.

"H" is the cross-sectional height of the valley walls,

and "W" is the cross-sectional width of the valley.

With that information, the concentration in a valley can be determined. For example:

Given a release rate of 10 curies per second, a wind speed of 7 meters per second, a valley wall height of 500 meters, and a valley width of 500 meters.

What is the concentration at 5 kilometers?

All the values need to be substituted in.

Then it can be solved.

The concentration at 5 kilometers is 5.7 times 10 to the negative 6th curie per meter cubed.

Dry Deposition

Deposition is the physical settling or placing of material onto a surface.

W-sub-d represents the surface concentration of curie per meter squared. This equation will be used to solve for W-sub-d.

This equation's purpose is to determine the concentration of radioactive material a plume leaves on a surface. The variable chi represents the plume's concentration over the surface, in curie per meter cubed.

V-sub-d represents deposition velocity, in meters per second. Deposition velocity varies depending on what is being measured.

EPA 400-R-92-001 deposition rates are as follows:

For Iodine, it is 1 centimeter per second, or 1 times 10 to the negative 2nd meters per second.

For particulates, it is 0.1 centimeter per second, or 1 times 10 to the negative 3rd meters per second.

"t" stands for the length of time the plume is above the given point at which you wish to calculate the deposition, in seconds.

All of the values necessary to solve for W-sub-d are available. For example:

Given an airborne concentration above the surface equal to 1.11 times 10 to the negative 5th curie per meter cubed, in a plume containing Iodine, over the area for 2 hours.

What is the surface concentration of iodine using the EPA deposition rate?

The deposition rate for Iodine is 1 times 10 to the negative 2nd meters per second, and hours must be converted to seconds.

All the values need to be substituted in.

Then it can be solved.

The surface concentration is 8 times 10 to the negative 4th curie per meter squared.

Estimating Concentrations Using Diffusion Graphs

An atmospheric dispersion coefficient log-log graph has been developed for each stability class: A–F.

When combined with this formula, they effectively replace the need to calculate concentrations using sigma-sub-y, sigma-sub-z, effective height, and fumigation graphs.

Chi represents the concentration of curie per meter cubed, or micro-curie per centimeter cubed. This equation will be used to solve for chi.

"Q" is the release rate, measured in curies per second.

Mu represents wind speed at the release height, which is measured in meters per second.

The value chi times mu over Q is found using the graphs, and is measured in meters to the negative 2nd power.

To use the graphs, first select the graph for the appropriate stability class.

For example: given a ground level release in a class D stability rating, with a wind speed of 7 meters per second, and a release rate of 3 curies per second, what is the concentration at 3 kilometers?

Using the D stability graph, move out 3 kilometers across the x-axis, and up to the H=0 line, to return the value 2.8 times 10 to the negative 5th meters to the negative 2nd.

Now, back to the formula.

All the values need to be substituted in.

Then it can be solved.

Chi is 1.2 times 10 to the negative 5th curie per meter cubed.

Estimating Distances for Concentrations using the Reduction Factor Table

Once a concentration has been measured or calculated for a specific distance and stability class, distances at which specified concentrations, or doses, would be found may be estimated by using this chart.

Care must be used when estimating doses using this chart. The release must be at ground level and there cannot be an inversion lid.

First, find the reduction factor.

For example, given a calculated dose of 5 rem at 5 kilometers from the release point, and a class F stability, how far from release would someone have to be to receive 1 rem?

Substitute in the values and solve to find a reduction factor of 5.

Look down the chart to find the reduction factor you calculated and look across to the applicable stability class column and determine the applicable distance ratio: 3.5.

To find the distance for the desired dose, we multiply the distance ratio by the distance at which the dose was measured.

Someone would need to be 17.5 kilometers from the source to receive a dose of 1 rem.

Minimum Requirements for Detecting Concentrations

NUREG-0654 requires that counting systems be capable of measuring radioiodine concentrations in air as low as 1 times 10 to the negative 7th microcurie per cm-cubed.
First, the minimum detectable limit must be calculated. Minimum detectable limit is measured in counts-per-minute.

The method used is different depending on whether the system involved is a digital system or an analog system.

For digital, only one piece of data must be obtained in order to calculate the Minimum Detectable Limit.

B is equal to the background, in counts per minute.

For analog, there is an additional requirement to solve.

RC refers to the meter time constant, provided by the manufacturer.

The detector's actual concentration measurement capability can be calculated, now that the minimum detectable limit has been determined.

The concentration is measured in microcurie per centimeter cubed, and sample volume is measured in centimeter cubed.

The count yield for this equation is measured in counts-per-minute over micro-curie.

Collection efficiency is the percent of the sampled material (in this case iodine) retained in the cartridge.

Detector efficiency is counts per disintegration. However, 2.22 times 10 to the 6th disintegrations per minute equals one micro-curie. We must use this in our conversion.

The necessary conversion: assuming a typical detector efficiency of 0.25%, or .25 count-per-minute for every 100 disintegrations-per-minute, converting the detector's count to a count yield in counts-per-minute over micro-curie involves the following conversion formula. (0.25% is a typical efficiency for GM pancake probes on a silver zeolite cartridge. A 1" or 2" NaI probe may have efficiencies near 10%.) We now have a number equivalent to (CY)(CE) for our system.

Now back to the equation, all of the values necessary to find "C" are available. For example:

Given an air sample volume of 60 liters per minute for 5 minutes, and a background count of 600 counts per minute, with a detector efficiency of 0.25 percent, and a collection efficiency of 90 percent, find if this digital system is capable of detecting the required minimum radio iodine concentration.

First the MDL must be calculated, so use the equation for digital systems.

Substitute in the background count, and solve.

The minimum detectable limit is 49 counts per minute.

The count yield must be converted to counts-per-minute over micro-curie with collection efficiency included.

Using the conversion equation, the count yield times the collection efficiency is 5.00 times 10 to the 3rd (5,000) counts-per-minute per micro-curie

Now back to the equation, all the values need to be substituted in, then it can be solved.

The system has the capacity of detecting concentrations of 6.53 times 10 to the negative 8th micro-curie over centimeter cubed.

It does meet the minimum requirement. If the required detection limit had not been met, then the sample volume should be increased to lower the detection limit. Sample volume should not be increased by increasing the flow rate because collection efficiency depends on the flow rate. It should be increased by extending the sampling time.

Determining Airborne Concentration From Air Sample

This formula can be used to calculate the airborne concentration of radioactive material from an air sample.

The equation solves for "C," which is concentration, measured in microcurie per centimeter cubed.

GC stands for gross count, measured in counts per minute, and BC stands for background count, also measured in counts per minute.

"CE" is the collector efficiency, expressed as a decimal. For a SilverZeolite cartridge, this is 90%.

"DE" is detector efficiency, also expressed as a decimal. For a GM Pancake probe with a SilverZeolight cartridge, this is 0.25%.

"ASV" represents air sample volume, which is found using a separate formula:

"t" represents sample time, in minutes.

"ASR" stands for air sampler rate, which you can find with another equation.

Air sampler rate is volume, in cubic feet, over sample time, in minutes.

Air sample volume is returned in centimeters cubed.

With that information, the airborne concentration can be determined. For example:

Given a gross count of 25,306 curies per minute,

a background count of 216 curies per minute,

an air sampler rate of 2 cubic feet per minute, for 5 minutes,

a collector efficiency of 0.9, or 90%

and a detector efficiency of 0.0025, or 0.25%

what is the airborne concentration of the sample?

The air sample volume must be found first:

Use the air sampler rate.

The air sample volume is 2.8 times 10 to the 5th centimeters cubed.

Now back to the equation, all of the values necessary to find "C" are available.

All the values need to be substituted in.

Then it can be solved.

The airborne concentration of the sample is 1.8 times 10 to the negative 5th microcurie per centimeter cubed.

Lesson Summary

Now that you've completed this lesson, you can:

- Calculate the concentration of radioactive material in situations including disparate factors:
  - Elevation of the release
  - Distance from centerline
  - Height of atmospheric mixing lid o Dispersion caused by large structures
  - Diffusion into a defined volume such as a valley
- Determine the minimum detectable limit for counting systems
- Utilize tools found in the EPA's Workbook of Atmospheric Dispersion Estimates (1970):
  - Atmospheric Stability Class table presented in this lesson.
  - Diffusion Graphs
  - Reduction Factor Table